JOHN SPARKS

THE SEXUAL CONNECTION

Mating the Wild Way

McGraw-Hill Book Company

New York   St. Louis   San Francisco

BY THE SAME AUTHOR

Owls (with Tony Soper)
Penguins (with Tony Soper)
Animal Design
Bird Behaviour
Animals in Danger
Island Life
The Air around Us

Book design by Barbara Hall.
Copyright © 1977 by John Sparks.
Illustrations copyright © 1977 by Spectrum Publishers, Utrecht, The Netherlands;
illustrations by Co Loerakker.

1 2 3 4 5 6 7 8 9 BP BP 7 8 3 2 1 0 9 8

Library of Congress Cataloging in Publication Data
Sparks, John.
The sexual connection: mating the wild way.
Includes bibliographical references and index.
1. Sexual behavior in animals. 2. Sex. I. Title.
QL761.S63 1977   591.1'6   78-17670
ISBN 0-07-059908-4

Contents

1
The Sexual Connection

In the life game, sex is the conjurer who juggles the chromosomes, shuffles the genetic pack, and deals fresh and sometimes winning hands to the next round of players. Sex emerges as the accelerator of evolution, since it steps up the rate at which changes can be made and so increases the chances of an animal producing progeny exceptionally well gifted to outcompete the rest of their generation. The sexual machine therefore bears the ultimate responsibility for the richness of life on earth, whether it be the dazzling colors in the tail of a peacock, the majesty of an oak tree, or the elegant grace of a Mozart symphony. Without the sexual connection, life might not yet have slithered from the primeval sludge.

This book is mostly about *mating,* rather than sex in the broad biological sense—and there is a difference. In everyday use, the two terms both imply intercourse. But strictly, sex refers to a way of propagating life through the cooperation of two kinds of individuals—male and female. "Sex" is about the *differences* between drones and queens, cocks and hens, bulls and cows, men and women. Some of the differences are clearly related to mating, which is itself crucial to the process of bringing sperm and egg together and so furthering the survival of the species. It seems natural to us that men should be equipped with an erectable organ, that women should have an extra hole between their thighs to receive it, and that both should derive pleasure from the process of placing one into the other. Yet the carefree way in which human lovers abandon themselves to each other should not conceal the truth that copulation is a serious business, and *must* be executed, at all costs.

Sex is a funny business. Nature drives us all to play the game, but when looked at in the cool light of day, rock'n'rolling on the deck is a comical way for otherwise dignified men and women to carry on. If it wasn't for the fact that bawdy love games arouse some of the best feelings in the world, probably none of us would be tempted to let our hair down. The sexual circus is pure ribaldry and mechanically awkward in the bargain. It has other drawbacks. Lovers of all kinds can be picked off by predators when their minds are on the job! Some males in breeding fettle are so one-track-minded about sex that by the end of their rutting periods they end up literally shagged-out, their survival prospects poor. For some animals mounting and mating can be a technically tricky maneuver, and even fraught with tension and danger. A bull elephant is brought to his knees in his efforts to make genital contact; the males of innumerable species make the supreme sacrifice, giving their life for love.

The strange thing is that sex and mating could be dispensed with; they are not absolutely necessary for breeding, as aphids and some kinds of celibate lizards show. For them at least, breeding is safe, simple, and less fraught—and certainly less fun. Nevertheless, the majority of animals are firmly sexual and play erotic games of some kind or other, and so the sexual process with all its bother must have something compelling going for it.

There is nothing like making love—or reading about it. We all have sex on the mind—some more than others. And we are as curious about the love life of animals as about our own. I know this only too well from my experience at the London Zoo. For several years I worked as a scientist there—a paid Peeping Tom, as it were, researching into the mating habits of birds and baboons. My own collection of animals housed in a laboratory could copulate to their hearts' content, away from the prying eyes of the visitors. But my work regularly took me out into the grounds of the zoo, where privacy gave way to public performance—in all things! I came to know what crowds around the lion cages meant. Leo was on the job—and frequently. When the black rhinos became passionate, visitors were in for a rare treat. Not only was their courtship as subtle as a contest between Centurion tanks, but the full splendor of the bull's yard-long weapon would make the onlookers' jaw drop. Once fully aimed and extended for a rear-guard encounter, the barrel had to be walked into the lover's inviting vulva, where it remained for more than half an hour.

The Victorian Primate House was no place for the prim. On the contrary, it proved to be a good stamping ground for the voyeurs of animal erotica. I remember copulating pig-tailed monkeys raising cheers of encouragement from a thrilled audience. The amazing blue crotch and vermilion penis of the male mandrill, shown off in full splendor, never failed to draw admiring glances from men and women alike. And more than once I saw pink-faced moms dragging their inquisitive little Willies past a relentlessly masturbating cebus monkey; not all the specimens on show obligingly revealed their all!

Many visitors pondered upon the difficulties of animal mating and raised the sort of questions that occur to all of us at times. I lost count of how often I was asked how a male porcupine copes. (The answer was always "carefully.") To be sure, the porcupine has a problem but, as we shall see, so have all animals when it comes to making the sexual connection.

Our inquisitiveness about how animals play the mating game is not mere prurience, because they are naturally at their most dramatic when they have sex on the mind. If I had ever had doubts about that, they would have been utterly dispelled by my work as a wildlife filmmaker.

Over the last ten years I have traveled widely, producing and directing natural history movies. Looking back over my hundred or so programs, the most compelling action sequences were often of animals directly or indirectly asserting their mating rights. I particularly remember some magnificent red deer stags with antlers like oak trees being transformed into battering rams by the whiff of a hind in heat. I came across similar scenes on the wide-open countryside of South Dakota, when the mighty bull buffalos turn from grass to more anxious thoughts. August was the rutting season and they had stopped roaming the prairies. Passions ran high between competing males, who banged their heads together and stirred up the dust.

Grass is the sole preoccupation of zebras for most of the day, but when a young mare is on the loose and smells seductive, the stallions go off their food in a flash. This happened several times while I was filming these humbug-patterned ponies in Ngorongoro Crater, Tanzania. While the adolescent virgin mare cantered through the crowds around a waterhole, she was keenly pursued by hot-blooded stallions, bucking, biting, and wrestling to claim her for their own. After watching calm family groups for so long, the action was thrilling and lent drama to the film. Although the fights were between males, the ultimate objective was copulation.

Mating of the kind that we are most familiar with is merely one of a whole range of exotic alternatives that animals have evolved for solving the central problem of how to fertilize their eggs. Every animal type has its own sexual strategy, and all are worthy of sensible investigation—tinged with a touch of humor: after all, fun is the very essence of our own sex lives. But our mating tools and tactics have not always been as they are today. Like the rest of our bodies and some of our behavior patterns, they have been arrived at through a slow but steady process of change which goes back to the very beginning of life on earth, because that is where our sexual connection has its roots. Compared to any one of our wild relatives, we may think that we play our love games to very flexible rules, in which everything goes. But there is little room for us to feel smug because, no matter what we are up to, some kind of animal was doing it in a similar fashion in the wild world a long time ago.

2
Supersex

We humans are the undisputed sexual champions of the world, the most persistently sexy of all beasts. Unlike most species, we have no closed sexual seasons, and women are as ready and able as men at most times during their five or more decades of physical maturity. Both sexes copulate as much (or more) for pleasure as for procreation, and that is unique in the animal kingdom. Female animals may get some kind of thrill from being served, but none experiences the spasms of intense sensation—orgasms—their male partners do. In contrast, during the course of human evolution women have been encouraged to enjoy mating by the development of their own sexual response that has an orgasmic kick to satisfy their passion. Our ever-ready sex drive reflects brains always open to new sexual ideas and stimulation. The two go together. In fact, to realize our potential in the mating game, it is helpful—and maybe essential—to cultivate a healthy interest in erotica.

Not that we have too much choice about that: it is hardly possible today to dodge the battery of aphrodisiacs that bombards us, from other people, advertising, and the media. The more explicit material we call pornography. Some people react to it as a thirsty man might to a desert mirage. Sex gourmands left unsatisfied by their torrid nights can seek inspiration and arouse their passions with erotic movies, which may fire the blood and stimulate the glands.

In normal life the ballgame is different. The chances are that you and I are less capable of hammering away at our birds like hungry woodpeckers until the dawn chorus calls us from our beds. Erotica may leave us with a niggling feeling that somehow we do not measure up. Nevertheless modern lovers with average anxieties and jealousies have an abiding curiosity about how their mating performances compare with those of others. A scientific survey prying into the frequency with which we put our private parts into action found that nine out of every ten people were sure that everyone else was having a better sexual life than they were. Animals have no such difficulties or anxieties. To that extent we qualify as the most sexually neurotic animal as well as the most sexually persistent. Indeed, more neuroses come to light when we turn to the tools of the mating game.

A lot of men have hangups over the size of their penises. Such anxieties are understandable because, after all, the penis and its ability to erect strongly is the very essence of "maleness." But sheer size has *nothing* to do with virility, although the old fallacies die hard. It is still widely held that great skill and stamina in lovemaking accompany a prize penis served by a pair of massive testicles. Lovers lacking in confidence, like bad workmen, blame their tools and try to improve on what nature has given them, driving themselves to impotence by massaging, pulling, and using various other methods to increase their penile measurements. Not that this is a peculiarly Western obsession. More gentle Eastern methods of elongation have long been available; the *Kama Sutra* has a number of exotic recipes, such as boiling up pomegranate seeds. Modern potions contain "hormone ingredients," but the offending penises stay much the same.

So how long should a penis be? Abraham Lincoln was asked a similar kind of nonsensical query concerning the length of a man's legs. "Long enough to reach the ground" was his answer. Although the penises of some animals can easily touch the ground, the fact is the human penis is designed to reach into the vagina, and providing it is long enough to achieve that target in a conventional mating situation, there is little point in its being longer. Even the smallest human penises are, once erect, up to the job for which nature intended them.

Penis length is something of an obsession with sexologists too, and numerous solemn surveys have been carried out in the name of science to see how far men vary. The longest and shortest are sported in Africa—by lanky Dinka tribesmen who walk nearly seven feet tall in the southern Sudan and by their squat pygmy cousins from the forested center of the continent. South African bushmen have the most unusual model: it never drops below the horizontal. On the whole, however, men differ less than you might think: small men do not necessarily have shorter penises than tall ones. Most limp penises hang for three or four inches, but the flaccid measurement is irrelevant because the organ is designed to do its work when stiff. During the process of stimulation it turns up and usually grows another couple of inches. An average man, therefore, has an erect penis just over six inches long and four and a quarter inches in girth, when measured just below the tip. The "average" penis is of course a mere mathematical mean. The majority of erect members are between five and seven inches long; eight-inch specimens are relatively uncommon, as are those that stiffen up at only four inches. Any that stand at less than four or more than nine inches are rare enough to be put in museums. This at least puts into perspective the stories perpetrated ad nauseam of enormous phalluses over a foot long. (With something like two billion grown men in the world, there are nevertheless bound to be a few exceptional penises around.)

The celebrated American sexologists William Masters and Virginia Johnson discovered that superpenises tend to behave differently from average-sized versions. Whereas normal penises increase greatly in size and go rock-hard when stimulated, naturally long limp penises tend simply to elevate and firm up. And the bigger they are, the less they are likely to harden. The resting size of a penis also has a bearing upon how much it extends. Normal penises grow by about one-third of their resting length as a prelude to lovemaking, but a three-and-a-half-inch penis may more than double its length, to as much as seven and a half inches, a 120 per cent increase. By contrast, a long dangling one resting at six inches or more will probably extend by only just over an inch when aroused.

There is a serious conclusion for sex-conscious people to draw from these facts and figures. No man should feel envious of the guy who has a great droopy penis: the premise that he has a huge erection is false. Nor should the owner of a small resting penis envy friends who are better hung, because when passions run high there may be little difference between their respective erections.

The penis serves to inject semen into the vagina; the effect of the lover's thrusting motion is to excite his woman by stimulating her clitoris and vaginal walls. Can a guy with a larger erection give greater pleasure than someone with only an average-sized one? Does an underendowed lover have to scrape the root end of his penis against his partner's pubis to satisfy her natural desire for penetration? The vagina is not a bottomless pit—the vaginal cylinder is only between three and four inches long during periods of sexual arousal. When stretched by the lover's penis, the tissues can yield to nearly seven inches or so, and then the experience starts to become unpleasant; few women could tolerate the stretching and pummeling of the ovaries that would result from riding on, say, an eight-inch penis. Therefore the length of a phallus over seven inches is largely wasted, because if rammed home completely it is more likely to cause pain than pleasure. And the vaginal barrel itself is only erotically sensitive for the lower third of its length—especially around its entrance. For the majority of women, therefore, the most arousing experience is to feel the portion of the penis working in the first couple of inches of the vulva. The rest is of minor importance. So a man with an erect penis measuring a mere three and a half inches could still make contact with all the right areas, with a thumblength to spare.

As Desmond Morris, my mentor at the London Zoo, has pointed out, man can be accurately defined as a naked ape with a big penis. Certainly in comparison to our nearest cousins we can be well satisfied. The chimpanzee has a mere pink spike, and the powerful gorilla is no better off. He would have lost credibility as a rapist ape long before he did if the perpetrators of such myths took penis size as a measure of virility. An adult male tips the scales at nearly 500 pounds, equivalent to the weight of three fully grown men, but has an erection only one-third as long as a man's, stretching just over two inches.

During the last century, European traders, explorers, and missionaries who had penetrated the mysterious hinterland of Africa reported stories of brutish apes raiding villages and carrying off native women to satisfy their lust. There is in fact evidence that steps were taken to conceal the anatomical realities of the male gorilla from the early days of its discovery. An American explorer, Paul du Chaillu, in 1861 published accounts emphasizing its ferocity and brutish appearance. He also claimed to be the first gorilla hunter and was therefore able to examine the animals closely, but he carefully removed the genitals before sending the dead specimens back to Europe. We do not know whether he mutilated the males out of modesty or if he wished to hide the unspectacular truth—that the male gorilla's tiny genitals hardly supported the superstitions he had helped to create.

Legends die slowly once firmly ingrained, and the idea that apes have enormous sexual stamina persisted well into this century. The monkey-gland business traded upon the belief that some of the ape's potency could be transferred along with its testicle into aging human males. Exaggerated claims were made in the 1920s by Serge Voronoff, who grafted chimpanzee testicles onto those of elderly men and noted their rejuvenation. The improvement in his clients was almost certainly wishful thinking, although Voronoff himself kept an especially large ape for himself against the time when his own glands started to fail.

The relative or absolute size of the genitals among different species has little to do with libido, and there is no biological reason why a poorly endowed ape could not abandon itself to a life of wild orgies. There is also no reason why it should. For a gorilla, a modest anatomy is in fact matched by a naturally undemanding sex life. Its details were not known until scientists went out virtually to live with the animals in the wild. George Schaller, an American zoologist, was one of the first, studying mountain gorillas in the dank bamboo forests around the Virunga volcanos in northern Zaire (then the Congo). The mature males are wonderfully impressive animals, with fairly long black shaggy hair on their limbs contrasting with a silver-gray body, but from Schaller's patient observations they emerged as gentle apes, spending most of their time chewing wild celery. In 466 hours only two copulations were noted, with one further invitation to mate not taken up. The heavyweight champion of all primates breaks no records as a sexual athlete.

Comparing and contrasting the sexual performance of animals with our own can be an entertaining exercise. But in playing the game it must be borne in mind that the contest is between unequals, and that each animal has the equipment and virility to fit its own special reproductive requirements. A gorilla's puny penis, when stiff and protruding, can inject semen far enough into the female gorilla's vagina to make her pregnant. If gorillas seem unsexy by human standards, they mate with sufficient frequency to maintain a healthy supply of infants and so keep their species going. The human penis in turn is unimpressive by comparison with that of some other mammals, but those who cast envious glances at a stallion's two-foot appendage should reflect that it would be as little use to the human lover as a man's would be to a horse in heat. If a sexually aroused animal has a long penis, it needs one: if another one has a short penis, that also is adequate.

For the biggest penises one naturally looks to the giants of the animal kingdom: big beasts need mating tools with a long reach. A stallion dangles his smooth black rubbery-looking penis two feet below his belly; a bull giraffe tipping the scales at well over a ton has a penis thirty inches long. Even barnyard bulls are literally designed for cowpunching, with a concealed one the length of a walking stick. When in the mood, he rears his mighty bulk onto the back end of a cow and thrusts his gristly pink rapier nearly three feet into her rump. The warmth of her vulva triggers him to ejaculate, and within a few seconds he slips from her back, his rod drawn back neatly into its sheath.

As you would expect, the African elephant is the champion heavyweight land animal, with bulls standing on average ten feet six inches at the shoulder and weighing five to six tons. (The size record goes to an enormous male that enjoyed life in Angola until 13 November 1955, when it had the misfortune to meet Valerie Fenykoevi, a Hungarian big-game hunter, whose admiration for the bull took the

form of pumping no fewer than sixteen heavy-caliber shells into it.
Its mountain of flesh weighed 10.7 tons, and when alive it must have
stood twelve feet six inches at the withers. In honor of its executioner
the bull is now called the Fenykoevi elephant, and is mounted in the
Smithsonian Institute, Washington. Visitors cannot, however, appreciate its genitals because elephants conceal their massive tools
and ten-pound testicles inside their bellies.) Only when the bull's
ardor is aroused by the sight and smell of cow elephants in heat does
the penis emerge, a jumbo package, sixty pounds in weight with
sufficient meat on it to fill a deep-freeze, and close to five feet long
when protruded. More interestingly, it is of unique design. Before
copulation, the great fat phallus is broadly S-shaped; furthermore, it
contains its own power-pack of muscles, enabling it to thrash around
searching for the cow's vaginal orifice and ultimately to probe around
inside.

In other ways, elephants are hardly the world's most ardent lovers.
Dr. Iain Douglas-Hamilton and his wife Oria spent five years with 450
elephants that inhabit the lush forests on the edge of the rift valley
in Lake Manyara National Park, Tanzania. During that period they
saw mating on only four occasions. The facts of the elephant's life
do not give him much hope of orgies. Cows only consent to copulate
for two or three days in the middle of their three-week estrus cycles.
That is the good news for the bulls; the bad news is that as soon as
a cow elephant comes into heat and is—invariably—inseminated, she
becomes pregnant and a devoted mother, which finishes her sex drive
for a further three or four years. Not surprisingly, when the infrequent
opportunity to mate does arise, the bulls are ready to go.

Nor do they make up for their relative celibate existence by a
lengthy courtship. A cow with the urge is quickly singled out, and the
bulls, which have established themselves a position of seniority in
the mating league, will often mount after simply laying their trunk on
their partner's back. Having waited for so long, speed seems to be
essential in their romance; for African elephants, copulation lasts less
than a minute, and with Asian elephants it appears to be even more
touch and go. Some American scientists working in Sri Lanka timed

their mating behavior precisely. On average a big bull spends 23.06 seconds up on the back of his mistress, while his self-propelled penis jerks around searching for its target; once homed in, he'll only enjoy it—if he does—for a mere 9.2 seconds. And of the sixty inches he has to spare, only the top ten usually manage to slip inside her. Brevity may be an expedient that has had survival value in such heavy animals. Mechanically, an elephant is stressed close to the limits of its supporting skeleton, and the weight of the bull must place an enormous strain on the cow's body structure. This may be why the cows of Asian elephants often brace their heads against trees or go down onto their elbows before taking a bull on their backs.

Living in water removes some of the constraints on size imposed on land animals. Whales are warm-blooded mammals and have taken mammalian sexual equipment with them from the land into the sea. Cushioned by water, they were long ago relieved of the need to bear their weight on a bony chassis and so have been free to exploit the advantages of being big. A large whale is a more efficient creature than a small one; it can keep warm more easily, and size for size needs relatively less food, being more economical on fuel when swimming. Such considerations have resulted in the evolution of marine giants, of which the blue whale is the greatest. It is perhaps the largest animal that has ever lived in the history of life on earth. The largest accurately measured individuals, slain earlier this century near the South Shetland Islands off Antarctica, were 109 feet and 107 feet long for a cow and bull respectively, and may have weighed around 200 tons each. The bulls have a penis that befits their monumental proportions, but it is not easy to see. The intimate details of whale unions remain hidden beneath the heaving surface of the sea, and at other times the penis is stowed away inside the animal's profile, in the interests of streamlining.

Sadly, the best chance to take a tape measure to a whale is when it is dead, and ready for flensing. At this time, the penis is often forced out of the body by the pressure of gases building up inside its decomposing body. Old engravings and woodcuts of stranded whales—such as sperm whales—often show them with their penises protruding. A blue whale's is so huge that it is folded away beneath the blubber in an S-shaped package; when it emerges from a big "blown" whale it stretches for between seven and eight feet. Of course it is not erect but, judging by the smaller dolphins, the limp one is probably not greatly different in length from the stiffened article poised for copulation—though it may be thinner.

Yet despite their supersticks, when sex begins to stir their blood—all 2000 gallons of it—the cetaceans set to work with an enormous drawback. Try putting yourself in the whale's predicament by making love in a swimming pool. But first you and your partner must climb into sleek and slippery wet-suits with your legs tied together and your arms clasped behind your backs. Now try having a whale of a time—if you can. Whales have no other choice; when their ancestors committed their bodies to the sea, the sexes had to evolve a way of linking up in water, and the long-reach penis must help.

If the world's prize penis must be the largest, the blue whale wins. But if we compare the *relative* penile sizes of different animals a very different picture emerges. A man's stiffened penis is nearly one-tenth as tall as he is. If reduced proportionately to the size of a man, the blue whale's erect phallus would shrink to between five and six inches—very similar to our own. Horses and elephants do much better, their erections approaching one-quarter of their body length when taking their legs into account. The champion penis, however, is found on an entirely different animal. To find it, simply go to the nearest shore, search for rocks or breakwaters washed daily by the tide and look closely: you will probably discover thousands upon thousands of chalky white spots—little barnacles, which have an incredibly extended sex life.

Barnacles are strange enough anyway. For centuries they were thought of as shellfish because they spent their lives cemented to the shore. Nothing could be further from the truth. On careful investigation, they have proved to be nowhere near the mollusks; they are really extraordinarily aberrant "shrimps," crustaceans. Although they begin as tiny larval animals drifting about in the plankton, later on a change of life overtakes them. Each becomes irrevocably stuck upside down on a firm surface. Enclosing itself in a miniature limestone castle, it makes a good living by straining food from the sea with its feathery feet and kicking it into its mouth. Sex on the seabed is full of strange twists.

Barnacles are hermaphrodites—each is equipped with both male and female organs—but like most ambisexual animals they do not like to do their own thing. To reproduce they need to copulate, like any other higher animal. As they cannot move around and search for a mate, they have come up with an equally satisfactory solution to the problem of loving their farflung neighbors. Each is equipped with a pair of snakelike penises of enormous proportions. The barnacle's body is merely one-quarter of an inch broad, but some species have delicate penises that can stretch nearly nine inches—over thirty times the length of the body. Although these little animals are usually crowded tightly together, they are nevertheless equipped for breeding in situations where they have settled sparsely. If mates are few and far between, a barnacle rolls out the full length of its penis and sets it roving around the rocks. If an invitation is extended by one of the distant neighbors, the fragile white tube slips into the shell and delivers some semen to fertilize the eggs. The recipient may then put its own penis into operation and make advances toward the first animal, so giving mutual satisfaction all round. If lusty men had a penis thirty times their body length, fifty yards or so, all sorts of possibilities (and hazards) would come within range—and remember the barnacle has *two* of them.

A shedfull of splendid tools does not make a handyman. Skill lies in knowing how to use them. So it is with mating. Record-breaking is about performance. Surely the top prizes in an all-comers sex olympics must go to two classes of lovers—those with the longest-running sex act, and those that can copulate most frequently. Animals with the most to shout about, like elephants and whales, are way down this scale of the lovers' league, as we have already seen.

Before turning to the mind-boggling abilities of wildlife, let us first determine a baseline for ourselves. It is a task beset with problems, because it takes two kinds of individuals—man and woman—to make love, and the potential performance of each sex is quite different. Another limitation is the difficulty of collecting records. Out of mankind's six billion, a mere handful of phenomenally fit athletes can cover a mile in less than four minutes; most would do well to run that distance in double the time. Likewise with sex. Some people are insatiable in their sexual demands and clearly don't go to bed to sleep. But sex maniacs are no more typical of the mainstreamers than are athletic freaks. So first, how often *is* often in human lovemaking? Many people self-consciously seek the answer to this question, but of course there is none. Couples make love as often as they like, and what is right for one pair may leave another frustrated beyond belief. Long-established lovers score an average of around two or three times a week. Plenty participate every night, and equally many set to only once a month. All are unexceptional. Admittedly, age takes an inevitable toll upon the virility of males—who go into top gear straight after puberty, when they are least deft in handling love affairs. Surging sex hormones from the newly commissioned testicles are at the root of this. When in their late teens, they have hair-trigger erections; the mere sight of soft feminine orbs swaying enticingly beneath tight sweaters and jeans is incentive enough. And when the chance comes to see what it's all about, many teen-agers can hold their penises erect continuously and ejaculate at ten-minute intervals. For most, such masterly performances do not last very long. As the years pass, men are less inclined to try for salvos of orgasms, and need more stimulation to rouse them. That is quite natural, but the desire for intercourse need never die completely. Sometimes the drastic falloff in lovemaking that people experience has less to do with withering organs than with boredom; even octogenarians are capable of girding their loins.

Adult men start at a biological disadvantage because ejaculation, which is for them the satisfying conclusion to a bout of lovemaking, effectively leaves them spent for at least half an hour. Sexologists who have been earnestly probing the mysteries of the male orgasm have discovered that men can be taught the techniques of controlling their body and so climaxing a number of times without releasing semen, but most modern males make it only once at a time.

That women can easily do better, if given a chance, is something that has begun to be widespread knowledge only recently, partly from scientific observation and to some extent as a result of a changing social climate in which human sexuality and the pleasure of both partners is increasingly seen to be both natural and healthy. Conditioning of the mind plays a powerful part in our sexual responses, which are generally what we expect them to be. The frigidity of Victorian ladies is an obvious expression of this. They were brainwashed into believing that copulation was an indelicate and unwholesome duty. It was for the benefit of the men. No lady of any breeding should give the slightest hint of enjoyment when her husband fumbled beneath her frilly nightdress and slipped in between her thighs. For these women it was simply a matter of gritting the teeth and thinking firmly of God and Country. With their heads filled with such distorted notions, few managed to let themselves go and experience the thrill of an orgasm with any regularity. Women brought up in less inhibited societies, and aware that sensuality and sexuality are good for them, rarely have any trouble.

Women have no such periods of depletion following climax as those men experience and are capable of moving directly on from one orgasm to another. During normal bouts in bed, relatively few (perhaps one in ten) women experience multiple orgasms; but in the sexologist's laboratory, a full performance can be aroused in "normal" women that would leave any virile man pooped.

The male's image of himself as being the super sex, with his pants significantly bulging, held in check only by the feeble hunger and endurance of the weaker sex, took a severe knocking when Masters and Johnson published the results of their researches. They were among the first scientifically to explode the myth that intercourse is limited by the woman's poor responsiveness. On the contrary. A few of the couples this team investigated were unusual in that the men were unable to reach a climax inside their mates' vaginas. They therefore were able to maintain an erection, and a state of intimacy for an hour or so, and during the extended copulation three out of five wives experienced several orgasms. But women can rarely achieve their potential during coitus. Those subjected by the experimenters to an orgy of mechanical stimulation recorded anywhere between twenty and fifty consecutive climaxes during an hour-long session. Each session was ended only when the women were exhausted. Yet their staying power was astonishing; they could undertake two to three sessions of sexual hyperstimulation like that each week, experiencing orgasm between sixty and 150 times. Such a level of excitement does produce internal effects, because the women began to suffer from chronic passive congestion of the pelvis and sorely enlarged clitorises. But it shows what women can do when relieved of the male's relatively poor erectile performance, which virtually limits *him* to three orgasms an hour—and three a day over a long period is a notable performance for a man in his prime!

How long can a bout of lovemaking be made to last—irrespective of orgasms? Mae West, not known for understatement, is said to have boasted that she once made love to a man called Ted for a fifteen-hour stretch. Most of us are contented with sessions that average out at somewhere between twenty and forty minutes—comparable to kangaroos, but far shorter than the marathon mating sessions of other Australian mammals.

With these facts in mind we can start our search for the sexual connection in the wild world.

3
Wild Sex

If there is precision in a name, then the screwworm would seem one with promise. Unfortunately, the screwworm itself is an impotent fly maggot which hatches in open sores on cattle. Christened because of their coiled shape, they are the scourge of cattle breeders, who do not approve of their habit of eating through steers. Sexual capability comes when the grubs finally change into flies. Although the female's performance is unexceptional—she copulates once during her three weeks of life—the males busily impregnate as many mates as possible from sunrise to sunset.

What about lovebirds, then? They do not make the grade either. These colorful little parrots spend long periods on the hors d'oeuvre but only occasionally reach the main course. Their name stems from the way they sit flank to flank, pressing cozily against their partners, billing and nibbling each other's head plumage. They symbolize sweethearts rather than sex bombs.

Lovebugs do a little better as symbols of lust. Like so many insects, they have short lives but passionate ones; they spend most of their five or so days before death romancing in the air. After about six months as grubs in the soil they emerge as adults rather like elongated houseflies, programmed only to find mates and copulate on the wing. This they do so well that the lovebug population is spreading down the Florida peninsula at the rate of twenty miles a year, and is now relentlessly moving in on Miami, where it arouses quite different passions in motorists. As the swarms of flies intent only on urgent promiscuity drift across the freeways, their clinched bodies become spattered on windshields and clog up radiators, overheating both the cars and their drivers. Such is the magnitude of the lovebug menace that a researcher was sent to find ways of dampening the lovebugs' ardor, so far with little success.

Rams have lent their name to ace sex performers. Their tupping season is usually held during the late autumn when ewes become fertile and ready to mate—but only with rams who have got to the top. For a month or two the rams are sex-crazy and devote nearly all their time and energy to achieving high sex status, to mate with as many ewes as possible. As each ewe comes into her two-day estrus period and becomes seductive, the heat is turned on the dominant ram, who guards them from the eager attentions of sex-starved outsiders. Every three hours or so he tups. Like many animals, rams mount their partners far more often than they ejaculate, because the act of repeatedly straddling and poking the penis into the ewe's vulva adds to the excitement. While in the mood, a ewe is generally mounted about twenty-five times, of which perhaps five or six are "takes" in which she is actually inseminated.

The athletic achievements of rams can be marveled at down on the farm, where the farmer sees that each one has a clear field and can enjoy the prospect of mating with thirty ewes at leisure, without bothersome competition from other rams. A ram in his prime can cover and successfully inseminate the thirty ewes in four days. If he makes twenty-five jumps onto each sexy ewe, he will be on the job no fewer than 750 times, and ejaculate on nearly 200 occasions over the course of the four-day period. The daily tally works out at 190 jumps, including fifty ejaculations!

Many hoofed mammals show astounding virility. The bull's performance has received a lot of attention because of his importance in the dairy and beef business. When stimulated with a succession of exciting cows, a bull can be driven to a sexual frenzy. One notable specimen, working in the interests of science, ejaculated no fewer than seventy-seven times in a six-hour sex session. Not that bulls are usually put to such strenuous tests or are inclined to that degree of potency during field trials. It is not in their interest, because when a male mates too often (and what that means depends upon the species) his fertility declines, defeating the whole point of the exercise—to fertilize females.

Wild animals, too, show great virility as a normal part of their breeding routine. Although capable of mating for at least six months of the year, red deer stags concentrate all their efforts into a relatively short period of autumn rut, when the does suddenly become seductive. The males are not out to break sexual records; they are concerned immediately with gaining status or property. It is the females who call the tune, and they are more likely to admire, and so be attracted to, males who have demonstrated their one-upmanship. A buck or stag in his prime who has a wonderful head of antlers and a good stamping ground will attract more mates than his less virile neighbors.

An antelope illustrates this. Each gorgeous orange-brown impala buck sports a pair of elegant lyre-shaped horns. They are also sexual gluttons—like most polygamous animals if given the chance. Between April and mid-May the males are in rut, carefully tending their own herds of hinds. Some manage to serve more wives than Solomon in all his glory; male impala have been observed herding as many as a hundred females during the mating season. Apart from the time spent in tupping with them all in turn, the buck is kept busy keeping the hinds on his turf, and warding off other jealous suitors.

Satisfactory sex goes with a desirable piece of real estate for the Uganda kob. These antelope live in equatorial Africa, where the balmy climate enables them to breed all year round. The females live in small herds, whiling away the days grazing and chewing the cud until they come into heat. They will then find the grass greener in what can only be called a red-light district. Among Uganda kob it is the males who disport themselves for the females to choose in a truly elegant mating system. The males of breeding age gather in traditional mating grounds and each strives for his own territory, about the size of a putting green, where he can offer the does a spread of grass like a well-laid dining-table. The attractiveness of an arena for the does depends on its position within the kobs' district. Those in the thick of the city are better than those in the suburbs. When mating time comes around, the slender long-legged females go gamboling for a guy with a good address. Picking their way through the peripheral territories and hardly giving a glance to the suburban males, they'll pause to graze in the center arena and allow the proprietor to mate. As a consequence every male kob tries to turn out the proprietor of the central territory and win a slice of the action himself. Should the top-ranking male wander off to drink or find food elsewhere, he may return to find his arena occupied and so have to expel the invader forcibly. His succession of lean black-eyed admirers also needs plenty of attention; despite their feminine grace and tender innocent looks, in the peak of estrus they are far from fragile and as randy as rabbits. At this time each visits the central arenas perhaps ten times a day and demands to be satisfied.

Few large mammals can compete with the virility of lions and their nympho mistresses. Crowned King of Beasts for their regal looks, lordly bearing, and power on the plains over life and death, lions could equally claim special status in the animal kingdom for their extravagant mating. They are not among the greatest movers on the savanna, but like all monarchs they regularly abandon their cool composure for carnal treats. Visitors to East Africa's fine game parks always make a beeline for the lions and more often than not find them dozing flat on their backs, legs spreadeagled, paws in the air. Complete exhaustion after a long night of hunting and killing? Not a bit of it— lions are like that for much of the night as well! Scientists who have watched prides around the clock have confirmed that lions spend about twenty hours a day sprawled out. However, this relaxed schedule goes by the board when a lioness in heat presents herself. Sloth-fulness abandoned, she repeatedly seeks out the company of males, rubbing and rolling sensuously in front of them and presenting her haunches: unashamed and intensely seductive behavior to which the males respond eagerly.

Fertile lionesses seem to be almost insatiable and copulate about every fifteen minutes for between two and three days; yet they are not wildly promiscuous, rarely changing lovers more than once a day. While consorting with an estrus lioness, a male devotes his entire energies to satisfying her sex drive and may be called upon to straddle her raised rump nearly a hundred times a day. There is no doubt about the male's ability to maintain such a formidable frequency. A courting lion was once watched continuously for two and a half days in the Serengeti. During the first day he copulated seventy-four times with one female and twelve with another. At the end of the second day the talley was further increased by sixty-two, and during the last half day he mated a further nine times. Thus over the course of the observation period the lion copulated a staggering 157 times, with an average interval of twenty-one minutes between mounts. While enjoying the pleasures of the flesh, the lion gave up his more usual interest in meat and did not eat. In wild prides a consorting male may get a raw deal over a lioness and become displaced after a day or two by a fresher and more rested colleague, but in the sanctuary of a zoo he has no trouble—or no respite. By the time the lioness' passion has subsided, a male may be prompted to mate 200 to 300 times. The record goes to a pair of zoo lions in Dresden known to have gotten together for eight days and copulated no less than 360 times. Little wonder that lions spend much of the period between their love-ins looking utterly zapped!

The big cats, however, would need a king-sized handicap to compete on fair terms with some of their smaller subjects. Admittedly, diminutive mammals live at a tremendous speed. Their body chemistry runs fast, and their natural lifespan tends to be short, so a whole lifetime of experiences and pleasures is crammed into a year or two. Sex is no exception.

Rodents are the recorded pace-setters, and the familiar hamster, a great favorite with children, is a hot contender. Hamsters are not fundamentally different from rats but are better shaped to encourage fond feelings: more rounded—therefore cuddly—flatter-faced, and without that long scaly tail that often arouses reactions of revulsion in people. At first experience the hamster appears a non-starter, sexually speaking; as most children know, when two are introduced they'll put up a display of fighting rather than lovemaking. A hamster likes a bit of elbow room and a bedroom to itself, and so in the cramped confines of a cage it is usually only possible to keep a single one— albeit a frustrated one. The females, especially, seek partners when they wish to mate, because a hamster in heat really has the urge to get up and go. Just how far they will travel during their fertile periods can be found out from the familiar treadwheels that are slung on the side of pet cages. If the wheel is fitted with a counter that records the number of revolutions, it can be seen that during a day—or more likely a night—the female hamster may well drive it for 100 to 200 turns; but when she suddenly comes into her passionate period, and her mind is firmly on finding a friend, then you'll hardly believe your eyes when you read the scale at breakfast time. Apply a bit of simple mathematics to the figure on the back of a cornflakes packet, and you may well compute that the now happily snoozing hamster padded five miles overnight. Had she found herself a hamster male, it would have been worth her while walking so far. During the first hour of their torrid meeting a pair will mate sixty-five to seventy-five times, an average of well over one mount a minute.

Top performer, though, is another rodent, closely related to the popular pet gerbils, called Shaw's jird. A pair of these appealing little mice made their record-breaking orgy before a reputable scientist, who counted no less than 224 mountings during the course of one hour! Not every one resulted in the release of sperm. Even so, the jird's stamina is remarkable even among mighty male mice, which do tend to be persistent and obsessive in their courting of estrus females. The puzzle is why some kinds are more vigorous as lovers than their relations of comparable size. Why should Shaw's jird be able to mate nearly once every fifteen seconds and a hamster about once a minute, while guinea pigs are satisfied by putting their hind ends together merely once an hour?

Of course, each jird's copulation lasts only about three seconds. In most mammals a high mating frequency, rather than long staying power, is the rule. As we have seen from the habits of the elephant, big beasts can be as brief in their loving habits as much smaller animals. Some notable exceptions have been recorded, however. Pigs stay together for anything between three and twenty minutes while the boar pumps up to half a pint (about 250 ml) of semen into his sow, the longest and most voluminous ejaculation known. But they can perform only four times a day. Their larger hippo cousins take a respectable hour wallowing in love. Kangaroos copulate continuously for fifteen to twenty minutes, sometimes longer. The male kowari, or Byrne's marsupial mouse, stays mounted for up to three hours, punctuated by brief periods of vigorous thrusting—between which the female usually sleeps! Stuart's marsupial mouse has an even more prodigious appetite for copulation, staying in place for twelve hours. Among lower animals, snails too stay in a mucilaginous embrace for up to twelve hours, and a pair of diamond-backed rattlesnakes were once timed in a love tangle for twenty-two hours forty minutes.

The agouti, a South American rodent rather like the guinea pig or cavy on slim stilted legs, is the only animal to better Mae West's reputed staying power. Agoutis are believed to remain coupled for about a day, though taking the animal kingdom as a whole even that does not qualify for a prize. Insects, of course, regularly stay in tandem for twenty-four hours, although the males only pass sperm for a short period. A pair of lovely sulphur-yellow brimstone butterflies was recorded locked in love for a whole week in 1919—a period of copulation that comes well within the scope of bondage, a subject to be discussed later. Any species that has evolved bondage techniques as a normal way of sex is bound to carry off awards for staying power. There is no shortage of animals for which sex is a full-time business.

Some of the world's top "sex maniacs" belong to a family of

parasitic flukes that includes the leaflike worms that ravage our livers and those of our domestic animals, causing a great deal of human and animal misery. The blood flukes are particularly interesting: the sexes only have to meet once in a lifetime, and it is then the worm's version of love at first sight. The larger male embraces the female, trapping her in a special groove, then plugs his penis into her tight little vaginal cavity, where it resides for the remainder of their lives. They exist in a state of permanent rapture, literally wrapped up together, bathed in the warm nourishing blood of their host "till death us do part"— meaning as often as not the death of their host.

The lifelong hug is deadly for about 100 million people in Africa and Asia, because the flukes use the abdominal veins as their tunnels of love and cause the disease bilharzia. The females make vast quantities of rather unpleasant spiny eggs which are extruded into the gut or bladder, depending upon the species. As a direct result the host may bleed, become infected, and develop cancerous nodules. Although the flukes can be assailed by all manner of medicines, once entrenched they are not easily removed, and the knowledge that the discomfort and danger is caused by incredibly sexy worms is little consolation to sufferers.

Threadworms can match any challenge made by the flukes. They are ubiquitous; one kind even has the good taste to live only in the felt mats on which German beer-drinkers rest their tankards. However, as with the flukes, it is the unpleasant side effects of their industry that attract human attention. Anemia and lethargy are the lot of people infected with hookworms; Jewish religious laws forbidding the eating of pork probably arose from deadly experience of picking up *Trichina* worms from pig meat. A massive dose of tiny *Filaria* worms in the lymphatic system results in grotesque enlargement of limbs, a condition called elephantiasis. Another hideous parasite, the Guinea worm, can grow to four feet long just beneath the skin, like a raised varicose vein secreting poisons. Many kinds of thread- or roundworms have sex in situ. One that goes by the name *Syngamous* needs a deep throat for its orgies, because it lives in the windpipes of birds and mammals. There the wriggling worms lead a life of continuous copulation. Each small male clings by his hind end to the female's genital opening, which he spreads by deploying vicious-looking spikes in order to maintain a good contact.

Find an animal that seems to be the ultimate in either beauty or extraordinariness and the chances are that another one surpasses it. The unpleasant—to us—little blood flukes and their ilk may live their lives as one long sex act; they live on the job. But they do not go quite as far as some males who are so utterly dedicated that they live inside the job.

At some time or other the females of most species seek the attentions of a loving male. The female *Bonnelia* is satisfied with nothing less than a male living blissfully inside her vagina. *Bonnelia* is not the kind of creature to set the world alight: it is a tiny green flatworm that snuggles beneath rocks on the seashore. But its sexual arrangements are as astonishing as anything to be found in the animal kingdom. The female is like a boarding house with one desirable room to let. When she becomes sexually mature, she advertises her vacant vagina, and the diminutive males take up residence inside her. For the favor of a comfortable and safe room, they fertilize the steady stream of eggs that pass through their accommodation—the ultimate in love-in husbands!

4
Solitary Sex

There is no reason you should have heard of the quahog. Nor is there any reason that a quahog should be acquainted with other quahogs, yet millions share the same bed. Each is snugly closeted behind limestone walls and is only dimly aware of what lies beyond it because it cannot see or hear, and its sense of touch is strictly limited. And with no brain worth mentioning, a quahog cannot indulge in a rich fantasy life of dreams to compensate for its state of worldly ignorance. It does not move much, and even feeding is an almost automatic accomplishment, microscopic crumbs being transported to the mouth on a slimy conveyor belt.

Yet there is one sensation that instantly rouses a quahog in its bed—the taste of another quahog's sperms. When these register, the otherwise placid creature becomes wracked with convulsions, ridding itself of its own cargo of spawn. It would be nice to feel that the creatures experience a kind of thrill or sense of satisfaction to relieve the monotony, but that isn't likely. Nor can they know the purpose of their twitching, or what caused it, because even in mating the quahog's bed holds no warmth of personal or emotional contact. The passionless quahog is a bivalve shellfish—rather similar to a clam—and as for many primitive animals the act that sets its sperms and eggs on the road to fertilization is a solitary affair, triggered from afar.

Traditional sexuality of the kind that we are all familiar with breaks down in spawners. Our way of love needs males who make sperms

and are built for transferring them to females. Females manufacture
eggs and are designed for receiving their lover's semen—one way or
another—and for looking after their brood. The labor of love is neatly
divided between the two sexes and is brazenly mirrored by shape and
mentality. But the anatomy of sexuality is less naked in bristleworms,
shellfish, sea urchins, and their kin. One purple sea urchin is very
much like its neighbor. A lugworm's-eye view is that one mate is as
good as another. You will look in vain at a coat-of-mail shell—a
chiton—clinging to the rock for signs of gender. In the manner in
which they launch their products into the world, there is often nothing
to choose between males and females. Their unisex image does,
however, conceal deep-down differences in their internal production
lines. Some are sperm-makers while the others are slaves to the egg
industry.

Spawning is the most elementary form of mating. It is also essentially
subaqueous sex, and mostly happens in the sea. The technique is cool
and simple. When ripe, the animals cast their sex cells into the water,
where they meet and fuse by chance. As a strategy to secure fertilization for a healthy proportion of the eggs, this nonchalant solitary
sex has its drawbacks. The sea is an enormous meeting ground, and
even in a rock pool the task for a short-lived sperm of finding its
female counterpart must be worse than looking for a dime on a football
field. Tidal rips may wash the fractions of spawn apart as often as mix
them. So how does this uninvolved kind of mating ensure the survival
of the species?

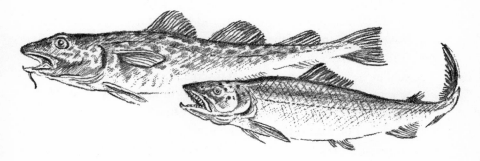

Some of the most numerous and widespread creatures in the world are soloists in the sex business. But they have modified their careless rapture to reduce some of the risks inherent in casting their spawn to the perils of the deep. It is no accident that virgin sturgeon, or ripe salmon for that matter, are bloated with millions of eggs. Their bulky ovaries simply reflect the incredibly poor chances of any one egg finally making it through to the finished fish. Prodigious production helps the sperms and eggs of solitary maters to get together; the sheer numbers defy the imagination. A cod that manages to escape being caught for fish sticks before her time is capable of making six million eggs during a breeding season.

American oysters can do even better. At a single laying, a female can liberate up to 115 million eggs, and she can repeat this staggering performance five or six times each season. Since oysters are not on the whole increasing or decreasing, this means that something like 700 million eggs have to be released by each female each year to raise the odds on a couple of them surviving to replace her and her unseen lover when they die. This huge production of sex cells is one of the prices animals like oysters have to pay for not looking after their spawn. (Compare it with that of a woman, who has an efficient technique for receiving sperm and who takes great care of her brood. She reaches puberty with only 10,000 potential eggs in her two ovaries, of which a mere 400 will be awakened, one a month, during the course of her reproductive life.)

Oysters are not unique in employing erotic chemicals to stimulate their mates to spawn. Simultaneous spawning is achieved in the same way by bristleworms, other shellfish, and sea urchins. Oysters often live crowded together on the sea floor—even in shell contact—and therefore in practice have little trouble in getting a taste of sex.

Sexual lunacy is perhaps the most fascinating way ever evolved to synchronize mates at spawning time. And, in keeping with occult images of promiscuity, the lunacy is more often than not combined with group sex on a scale that leaves our wildest orgies looking feeble by comparison. Those who live in Bermuda are familiar with the moonlit flits of fireworms. These are marine cousins of our common garden earthworms, but their bodies are equipped with a series of hairy paddles that help them get a grip on the water. For much of the year they live like respectable worms, scavenging food on the sea floor; then suddenly their sexual hunger causes them to light up at night and head for the sky. Their mating periods are impeccably and literally managed by moonshine, because ripe fireworms only swarm and spawn during a few evenings following the full moon. Fifty-five minutes after sunset—give or take a few minutes—the first fireworms wriggle forth into the inky blackness of the ocean. Within seconds the rest of the worms, glowing with excitement, pour from every nook and cranny of the sea floor. The nuptials take place beneath the rippling surface, under the silver glimmer of the waning moon. Not that they need help from the heavens to illuminate the scene, because each worm can see and be seen. The planktonic rendezvous has the enchantment of a Disney ballet, with the fireworms flashing and making trails of stardust to mark their course through the water. When ready to spawn, the glowing females swim in tight circles and leave some of their light behind in the water and on their eggs. This lures groups of winking males, who dart to and fro through the females' luminous wake. While dancing and weaving beneath the waves, the mates are excited by each other's erotic chemicals and discharge their spawn in each other's tracks. Within half an hour the living lights have faded, and all that remains of the fiery mass mating are countless millions of tiny transparent spheres drifting through seaspace. They contain the germs of the next generation of fireworms.

Swarming and lunacy are both methods worms use to improve mating efficiency. As for sea urchins and clams, fertilization is still an outside event, but by seething together and coming close to each other, mating bristleworms help their sex cells to meet. Gearing such get-togethers to the rhythm of the moon is a sophisticated refinement that makes specially good sense to breeding marine animals, even if it seems a trifle eccentric to landlubbers.

Although a quarter of a million miles away, the moon is still close and large enough to tug powerfully at earth's watery shawl, releasing the grip when she turns her face away. Every drop of fluid on our

planet responds to the force. Sensitive instruments can record tidal movements even in a teacup. If the moon were fixed in the sky, the earth would rotate beneath her bulging garment and bring a tidal surge to every shore at twenty-four-hour intervals. However, the moon is in motion, and it takes us an extra forty-eight minutes each day to catch up. High tides therefore arrive forty-eight minutes later each day, so that the daily tidal cycles are ever drawing apart, then coming inevitably together again. Irrespective of whether it is light or dark, shore animals take their time from the tides. Their "day" is divided between periods of flood and periods when they are left gasping for water.

(The sun's gravity is also strong enough to pluck at the oceans, and during these two periods it lends its support to the pull of the moon.

For a day or so, twice each lunar month, the strong, surging spring tides flood the seaboards, their ebb leaving the shore extra high and dry. In between, when the heavenly bodies are at all angles and the moon is in its quarters, the tidal range is diminished; we call these small tides neaps. Spring tides are particularly significant to spawners, which rely upon a vigorous movement of water, both to mix their sex cells and to transport their planktonic embryos far and wide to fresh sea pastures. Precision is often crucial.)

Preparing for sex on the tides means using the *light* of the moon as a timekeeper, rather than the periodic passage of huge amounts of water. This is the more remarkable because full moonlight is 300,000 times less intense than the glare of the sun, and moonbeams are further dimmed by their passage through the water. We know that light from cosmic lanterns plays an important part in arousing animals sexually, as a couple of examples will show. The gradually increasing amount of daylight after the winter solstice stimulates many birds to mate and puts a spring song into their voices. In the forests, the spring-dawn chorus makes way in autumn for the roaring of rutting red deer. Their sexual equipment is brought into working fettle by the steady shortening of the day. The stags are so sensitive to the duration of daylight that their testes start manufacturing sperms only a couple of days after the summer solstice.

Primitive sea animals, then, are not the only ones whose passions are aroused by lunar rhythms. Some members of the terrestrial night-club also have their sex drives geared to moonlight. We are familiar with the notion that cats tread the tiles when the night is lit up, and that dogs bay the moon. Bats, particularly tropical ones, spend the daylight hours asleep, and only emerge from their caves or hollow-tree roosts a few minutes after sunset. Also, where many of them live, the duration of the day and night are much the same throughout the year. Perhaps they take their mating time from the moon; certainly the mating periods are so precise that some kind of timekeeper must switch the bats on to sex with the punctuality of a clock striking midnight. Southern long-fingered bats, which live in the New Hebrides, only mate during the first five days of September. Fruit bats in Sri Lanka put their upside-down ends together during September. The effects of the moon on the nightjar, a bird of the twilight, hunting moths and other insects on the heaths of southern England during summer, are accurately known. Its arrival is signaled by the cock's churring song that starts up after sunset and advertises his readiness for sex. His mate waits for the moon. She copulates and lays her eggs during the last quarter of the lunar cycle, so that her chicks will hatch during the next full moon, when hunting can continue all night. If the eggs are stolen early in the incubation period, three weeks will elapse before a new clutch is laid, so bringing her back in phase with the moon.

Not that we ourselves are immune to the influences of the moon, even in our sex life. When human lives were ruled by myths and magic, not so long ago, the waxing and waning of the moon were thought to influence everything. A growing moon emanated strength and luck. Farmers therefore planted seeds so that the young crops were breaking the ground during the period of the waxing moon. If they put sense before sex, young lovers planned their marriage and subsequent "honeymoon" for the time of the enlarging moon, to derive full benefit of the lunar force. But moonlight had its dangers. Those who fornicated beneath the silver glow of the full moon did so at their peril, because fairies, witches, and evil spirits were fond of walking the woods on such nights. Women also widely blamed the moon for their pregnancies.

This belief lives on in the idea that the lunar rhythms control fertility, through the menstrual cycle. But a woman's ability to round off a session of lovemaking with an orgasm also varies with the menstrual cycle. It peaks out about halfway—at ovulating time—subsequently falling off sharply, and then perhaps surprisingly surges to a new peak just before menstrual flow. So, *if* the moon influences menstruation, it also indirectly controls the capacity for enjoying intimate relationships. That the moon and menstruation should become mixed up in the minds of superstitious people was probably inevitable, since roughly four weeks—a lunar month—elapses between periods.

Back in the sea, there is a sound reason for bristleworms, sea urchins, and many fish to develop sexual lunacy; it helps them "forecast" the most propitious time to release their sex cells, when there is an abundance of water or a glut of mates. There is no convincing explanation why human sexuality should have been geared to lunar cycles.

There can be no doubt about the steady improvement in mating efficiency made by the fishes. Even the solo performers manage their sexual releases in such a way that fertilization is achieved with little—if any—wastage. Take the European stickleback, perhaps the most intensively studied wild species in the world. Adult sticklebacks are only a couple of inches long, but sexy males can afford to be flashy, with a fiery red belly, sparkling turquoise eye, and pale green-blue back, and sport themselves out in the open: they are protected by an array of vicious spines. Their unvarying mating routine is carried out in spring in shallow pond or river water. The male first builds himself a small "tunnel of love" out of weeds on the river bed, and then goes looking for a wife. He recognizes a suitable female because she is all silvery and shiny, and nicely bloated with spawn. By darting to and fro in front of her, he patiently leads her down to his mating pad and shows her the entrance by pointing it out with his nose. When she has wriggled inside, the male excites her to spawn by gently ramming her rear. Less than a minute later the female has finished and slips away. Her bright-eyed suitor takes her place and ejaculates a drop of milt over her cluster of fifty to a hundred eggs. His emotions are now quite different toward his spent and flattened lover. She lost her sex appeal along with her eggs and he attacks her if she hangs around. As soon as he puts his house in order he will be back at the game, luring another four bulging females one after the other to his nest until a sufficiently large clutch of eggs has accumulated.

Mating or spawning in sequence is the fate of huge numbers of fishes, although the details differ between species. Among salmon and trout, for instance, the larger hens plow troughs in gravel stream beds with their tails. When each is ready to spawn, a cock or two cocks moves in and lie close to her, in a position to squirt sperm over the eggs before she covers the cache with a flick or two of her tail.

Simultaneous spawning is in fact the commonest mating strategy in fish.

Sex starts in schools for colorful surgeon fish. As for many other shoaling species, togetherness is a way of life for them. They spend most of the day drifting around coral gardens in shoals, browsing off seaweed; when threatened by a voracious shark or grouper, they seek closer comfort than usual and speed off in a compact bunch. In keeping with their sociable nature they also practice group sex. At mating time the fish hold erotic parties, where they mill around in a frenzy to find spawning partners. When the surgeons can contain themselves no longer, groups of up to five break away from the crowd and, keeping close formation, swim rapidly upward for perhaps five feet, then abruptly dive back into the party. At the peak of the movement, the fish simultaneously reach their climaxes and leave behind them a small cloud of spawn. Although the sex is social, mating still does not involve any bodily contact.

Cod at least have made an important move toward the closer kind of copulation that appeals to most of us. A cock cod has no clue who his lover will be until she suddenly slips into his part of the seabed and shows signs of staying a while in response to his passes. Gliding to and fro with flashing fins, he flaunts before her, gently nudging her now and again, even crooning to her, cod-style. If she swoons at his grunting courtship, she will follow him to the end of the world—which means the surface of the sea. That is where the male leads her, and that is where his problems start, because he must then execute a couple of delicate mating maneuvers that will bring their vents close together before simultaneously releasing their sexual products. First the hen becomes still, and the amorous cock mounts and embraces her with his pelvic fins, so they are both in contact, one on top of the other. He then slips down one side but still keeps hold of her until he comes to lie almost underneath, with his belly and genital aperture pressed to hers. This is the signal for spawning. Once in position, eggs and semen stream from the pair of cod. Contact is made between lovers, but their mating is essentially coupling and not copulation, because the male has no way of entering his mate's sexual avenue and depositing his semen inside her.

So it is too with frogs and toads, but their coupling is more tenacious than the flimsy embrace of the cod. They have developed piggyback sex in a move to increase their mating efficiency. The clawed toad, which lives in marshes and rivers in South Africa, prefers not to venture onto the land unless forced to by summer droughts and is accordingly especially well equipped for swimming, with a pair of powerfully muscled hind legs which sport equally large flippers. Its chief claim to fame has been its role in divining pregnancy from a woman's urine. During the latter half of the 1920s, the only method of confirming whether a woman was pregnant or not was to inject some of her urine into a female mouse. Pregnant women excrete large quantities of sex hormones—gonadotrophins—via their kidneys, and these will affect the ovaries of other animals. After five days the mouse was killed and its ovaries minutely examined for signs of being stimulated by injected gonadotrophins. If positive, the lady was declared pregnant, if not she could either start again or be more careful next time. In 1931 researchers working in Cape Town discovered that a female clawed toad given a shot of urine containing sex hormones would respond by obligingly discharging its eggs between five and eighteen hours later. The agony of waiting was reduced for the clients, and the toads could be used time and time again. Clawed toads were suddenly in demand and were exported all over the world to hospitals and pregnancy-testing laboratories. Male clawed toads are also in the testing business, their problem being to sort out the hot females "pregnant" with eggs from the rest.

When in the mating mood male toads grow spiky pads on their hands, which help them to take a slippery female from the rear and grip her tightly in the groin. Their method is simple sexual assault. A male raring to go is quite indiscriminate about whom he tackles, and makes a grab at anything that moves. His trial-and-error technique guarantees that he will not miss a chance at mating. However, as often as not, he first gets his arms around another male or a cold unreceptive female, or even a lump of mud that looks the size and shape of another frog. Mistakes are quickly corrected—certain clues make him back off as if doused with cold water. A male firmly clasped round the thighs by another male will croak his displeasure. Nor is there any point in passionate males hanging onto cold mistresses: unready females do not take kindly to being encumbered by a male and tut-tut their annoyance. It is a waste of time for the male to wait for her mood to change, so he lets her go. If the partner does not protest, the male knows that he is on to a good thing, and rides around on the back of his hot female until she is ready to spawn.

This piggyback mating is contrived to keep the couple's vents close together during the process of spawning. As the eggs begin to emerge, the male digs his snout into his partner's spine and arches his back to bring his hole as close to hers as possible. A gutter forms in his belly and the emerging eggs funnel down it to his vent, where semen is duly sprinkled over them. When she has shot her eggs, she quickly loses interest in sexual contact. The embracing male finds her repulsive and dismounts to look for yet another coupling partner. This is the mating pattern in the vast majority of toads and frogs, although the details vary between species.

Amphibians such as toads have made a great evolutionary breakthrough by being able to survive on the land. But their conquest is incomplete, since their mating and breeding routine remains geared to water. Many ingenious solutions to the problems of providing water or moisture for their tadpoles have been developed by terrestrial toads, and a few of these involve very strange mating techniques.

Foam frogs use group sex in a bubble bath. These frogs live in trees, often around swamps and marshes. They have dispensed with sex in the water, and package their eggs in nests of foam which they construct in foliage above pools and puddles. When the tadpoles hatch they wriggle free of their bubble nurseries and drop into the water, where they will continue their childhood. The foam frogs mate in the cool of the night. When a female finds herself a suitable spot above water, she is quickly sought after by the local males; they are smaller than she is, and she can, and often does, take on several. The first clasps her under the armpits, the next rides on top of the first mate and so on. But all these spawners can enter into several biologically meaningful relationships simultaneously because they are not limited by the demands for anatomical docking. A gluttonous woman indulging in anal intercourse and fellatio as well as the more straightforward form of loving can, presumably, have a group grope with three men at a stretch; but the female frog can huddle with as many males as are available, because they all go solo at the climax of their sex act. She starts the ball rolling by producing a pale translucent fluid from her rear, and immediately she and her multiple lovers set to work whipping up the fluid into a stiff white foam with their hind legs. It looks like an erotic cooking session, semen and eggs being folded into the mixture to make a kind of meringue for the benefit of the children. After a short while the mating frogs are nearly covered in froth. When the female is spent the group disperses, leaving between 100 and 200 eggs behind in the foam. The outside sets fairly hard, sealing in the soft moist center into which the tadpoles hatch.

The mating ritual has come a long way from that of the solitary quahog. Frogs are spawners, but unlike shellfish they have taken the solitariness out of sex by coupling.

5
Packaged Sex

The mechanical injection of sperm to fertilize female horses, sheep, and dogs was practiced in Arabia as early as the fourteenth century and is far from uncommon on dairy farms throughout the world today. When a developing medical science made artificial insemination of women possible, a hue and cry concerning legality and ethics arose—especially among those who had no need of it. Human artificial insemination involves using prepackaged semen, usually from an unknown donor, to assist in conception and is being used more and more frequently by couples who cannot otherwise produce children. Delivering and receiving semen in containers has to do with procreation, not pleasure, but packaged sex is a perfectly normal mating routine for a surprisingly large number of animals. Indeed, our own very primitive ancestors may have been members of the club hundreds of millions of years ago.

Exponents of packaged sex are everywhere, even today. When the scorching sun disappears behind the cacti and the air cools, scorpions emerge from their lairs to have sex on the desert sands. They are rarely overtaken by the desire to make love—even scorpion style. The female shares the reputation of her sex with her mate: *both* are deadly rather than lovable; they need to be, because they are voracious hunters. They have solved the problem of killing their victims by injecting them with a shot of lethal venom from their tails. Within seconds of a strike, a cricket or lizard is paralyzed and the powerful poison starts dissolving its tissues, thus making the scorpion's meal easier to eat. A scorpion behaves like a machine programmed to intercept prey and devour its own weight of food each day. It grabs, and lashes out its sting, at anything that moves. If threatened by something too big to tackle, it just as readily uses its needle for defense. Sex is therefore potentially a hazardous affair where each partner has to avoid ending up as a meal rather than a mate.

The scorpion's answer has been to develop a technique of mating at arm's length. The lovers approach each other gingerly with open arms, but the embrace has no warmth for either: the "hands" are just massive claws designed to seize and tear their victims apart. The courting couple disarms itself by clutching each other's claws and leaving their venomous tails very much behind them. The male then leads his murderous female on a merry dance around the rocks until he finds a suitable spot for the next stage of his mating ritual. He somehow has to bridge the gap between his and her genital openings so he can fertilize her eggs. He does this by sending her a kind of love letter—a neat package of sperms. Holding her firmly, he sticks what looks like a tiny white bottle into the ground: a container full of sperm. He then carefully walks backward, maneuvering the female so that the open lips of her genitalia are drawn over the thin neck of the package. If he guides her correctly, she scoops up the sperm parcel and becomes impregnated. Once she's got what she came out for, she switches to the hunting mode. Accordingly the male lets her go and makes a quick tactical withdrawal. By the time the sun begins to bake the desert once more, she will be in her relatively cool cellar, digesting the victims of her night's hunting, while her mate's sperms enter the eggs deep inside her body.

The scorpion's sex act is a distinct advance on anything we saw in the last chapter. It has also been going on for a very long time, because the fossilized remains of terrestrial scorpions have been unearthed in rocks 400 million years old, from the Silurian period. Scorpions must therefore have been in the vanguard of life as it spread across the dry land. Perhaps their method of mating contributed to their success as one of the first pioneers.

Having become committed landlubbers who drown in water, it is difficult for us to appreciate the achievement of the first faltering steps animals took away from the primeval swamps. On our planet the sea was the cradle of life, and so from the beginning all living things have been hooked on water. For a billion years—almost an eternity—animals flourished only in places where their bodies could be bathed in water. The breakthrough into the drying air was accomplished by the evolution of sophisticated life-support systems.

Survival on land also required a sexual revolution. Spawning is an ideal if rather wasteful form of subsurface sex, but it is useless away from moisture, as terrestrial toads show. Burdened with the technique of their fully aquatic ancestors, they must seek out ponds when they wish to mate. Even those toads that live in deserts must wait to couple until water lies around in puddles; so toads are not too common in hot dry places. But desert scorpions have a high-and-dry sex life with no such restraints. Like all successful land colonists, they have undergone the mating revolution and come out of it as advanced animal lovers thoroughly emancipated from water. Oddly enough, the male's method of bundling semen before passing it to the female may have been perfected by his aquatic forebears as a strategy for reducing sperm wastage; it would have made the subsequent move onto the land that much easier. Although a few scorpions live in moist, humid places, the fact that some manage to survive and thrive in the driest deserts in the world testifies to the success of their sex technique. A few moments in warm air would be sufficient to dry out a droplet of scorpion semen and shrivel the sperms to death; sealed up in their own private pond they can survive being passed between the couple until they are released into the wet reproductive tract of the female.

And these venomous little creatures had perfected their sex act over a hundred million years before our reptilian ancestors "invented" the penis, which was essentially the vertebrate passport to terrestrial sex.

Male scorpions are not alone in presenting sperm parcels to their mates. Many other animals have independently evolved a similar sort of sex. Some leeches (which, like most blood-sucking parasites, get a bad press) have a method of mating which to us appears as revolting as their vampirelike table manners. Take duck leeches that live in the mouth and nasal passages of wildfowl, often in such numbers that they cause the host to die of suffocation. When a duck leech feels sexy, it lopes off in search of a partner. Compared with the task of the courting scorpion, its love life is plain sailing. There is no careful ritual to observe, no sensitive spots to be contacted or inviting orifices into which the package must ultimately be popped. Once the roving leech has found a receptive sucker, it wraps up a bundle of sperms— technically called a *spermatophore*—and plants the package any- where on the partner's body. The sperms gain access to the eggs in what appears to us a highly painful process. The spermatophore releases cell-dissolving substances, so that the skin around the sperm package ulcerates. Slowly the bundle containing the male sex cells sinks through the skin. Once inside the leech's "belly," the sperms are finally liberated and wriggle around the internal organs until they reach the eggs.

There is evidence that this casual style of lovemaking is of great antiquity, because stick-on sex is employed by a primitive southern-hemisphere land dweller called Peripatus, which resembles a rather pretty velvet walking worm sporting about twenty pairs of short baggy legs. The male has an odd style of stick-on sex.

The way to the heart of a female Peripatus is not through her belly but literally by way of her bloodstream. All the male has to do is go for a stroll and place a sperm capsule at random on his lover's long, sinuous body. Where he sticks it is immaterial—sometimes it lands on one of her forty fat little legs. He may be careless to whom he gives his precious presents; he even approaches other males, and woos barren young females who have no chance of giving birth to his children. Biologists puzzled over how the sperm managed to reach the female's eggs until it was discovered that tissue-engulfing white blood cells in the female's body migrate to the spot beneath the sperm capsule and start to excavate a passage in her body wall. Meanwhile the base of the spermatophore begins to break open and the mobile sperms wriggle through the female's bloodstream, which then transports them to the ovary. Once there in force, they break through into the eggs.

If the lovemaking of Peripatus looks haphazard, so is that of lower forms of true insect life. In fact, impregnation seems to be a purely accidental process. Take the diminutive springtails, which are not only ubiquitous but phenomenally numerous. An acre of English meadowland can support over 250 million. Some even live on the snows of Antarctica and the Himalayas, where they thrive on wind-blown pollen. Although true insects, they have no wings but launch themselves into the air rather like fleas, using a unique lever system tucked under their tails. Courting is a simple business. The male needs no prompting from a female, and leaves behind him droplets of semen on stalks, rather like pins in a pincushion. With so many springtails crowded together, sooner or later a ripe female is bound to blunder into the spermatophores; they break open and she collects the fluid semen as she rubs her rump against the burst capsule.

The male water-springtail does actually select a mate and gives her a little guidance. He is by far the smaller of the two and can be recognized by the structure of his feelers, which are shaped like tongs and used for keeping ahead of his bulky mate. Facing the female, he grips her antennae as though they were the horns of a bull and is carried around like a half-tossed matador until mating time. After dropping his spermatophore, a tug of love takes place. Straining with all the might of his six legs, he drags his mighty mistress over the semen droplet, which she takes up with her sexual pore.

The closely related bristletails might appear to have fun and games when mating. Most of us are familiar with these little silverfish, with gleaming coats of silvery scales, that live as uninvited guests in our own homes and have a taste for crumbs and books. Their sex life is discreetly hidden behind the baseboards. In the presence of a mate, the male lays his spermatophore, giving away its location by spinning silken love lines over the spot. The female trips around and beneath the threads but is brought to a halt as soon as her back touches one. This signals that she must be standing over the sperm parcel, and she accordingly lowers her "belly" rhythmically to the ground until her vent makes contact with the droplet. Another species of bristletail has a different mating game: he makes mating beads. The courting male anchors his love line, and as he slowly draws it out deposits his sperm droplets like beads on a thread. He does not let go of the cord, but holds the line taut with the tip of his tail, at the same time wrapping himself around the female. He then gently shoves her backward until her tail bumps into the beads.

Both bristletails and springtails are in a sense living fossils, early insect models which were around long before their more familiar relatives like bees, beetles, and butterflies had evolved. Many of these illustrate the next stage in sexual sophistication, the male obligingly giving the sperm packet to his mate and introducing it safely into her sexual orifice. To achieve this the lovers need to strike up a more intimate relationship, involving a degree of body hugging and genital contact. That you may think is natural progress, from the lonely little springtails sadly dropping and bumping into sexual pin-cushions to copulation of a kind—which may be fun even for insects. But the pursuit of pleasure played no part in bringing insect lovers together in a sexual balancing act. Once again, it was biological efficiency that prompted the steady move toward linking the lovers. After all, many spermatophores planted by a male springtail go to waste, and even a female scorpion with a "chivalrous" male to guide her often misses a sperm packet or two. By direct posting into the vagina or some other female sexual zone, a male gives his sperms a much better chance of seeking out the eggs. Most insects and crustaceans have come this far.

While terrestrial insects were forging the way toward their own kind of copulation, back in the sea male crustaceans were perfecting a bizarre method of coupling with their feet. Most of us appreciate the tender rump ends of the Norway lobster, because when chopped up, buttered, and browned they are often served as a substitute for scampi. Alive and kicking, these relatively small lobsters are attractive cream-and-orange animals that are trawled from the sea floor over large areas of the European continental shelf. (No fewer than 51,000 were taken from the Irish Sea for a scientific exercise to sort out their reproductive life.) Anyone who has peeled shrimps or tried to crack open a crab's claw must realize that a crustacean's body—like that of any arthropod—is constructed quite differently from our own. It has a soft center, with all the protective and strengthening skeletal material on the surface, like a crust. Male and female lobsters therefore resemble medieval knights clad from head to foot in jointed armored plating, with hardly a chink left to expose the yielding flesh underneath. Without the crustacean equivalent of a can opener, how can lobster lovers drop their guard and expose themselves to each other? In fact, lobsters periodically go weak at the knees and turn soft. This happens during their short spurts of growing, when they cast off their tight shells and secrete an elastic suit, which hardens up after a day or two's growth.

Male lobsters mate when they are firm, but they are only interested in soft females, packed with eggs; these show their readiness to copulate by exuding an exciting taste from their bodies. The males of some species, impatient for sex, even help their intended lovers out of their old "clothes." Like all large crustaceans, a female lobster is not designed for receiving sperm parcels directly into her genital tract but has a cubbyhole for them beneath her "chest." This thelycum is essentially a holding compartment formed by an inward denting of the crustacean's chalky skin. When her armor stiffens up, the aperture is all but closed, and so the male can probably only force an entry when his lover is soft and pliable. He does this by dipping one of his many toes into her sperm compartment.

A male lobster is indeed a lesson in legs and what they can be used for. Some are small, for manipulating food into the mouth; one pair is massively constructed as a set of pinchers. Those beneath the chest are long and spindly for walking, whereas the appendages beneath the tail are mostly for swimming. Between these two sets midway along the body are two pairs of short spindles called pleopods, the front set being hollow like a couple of straws. The male lobster boasts a pair of penises, a right and a left one which emerge just behind his chest; but they are not long ones, and so when the time comes for mating these pimples project into the base of the hollow pleopods— rather like a man's penis hanging down his trouser leg; the leg shafts give the male lobster the reach. The second couple of pleopods come forward to stiffen up the accessory penis and help it to penetrate the lady's cubbyhole.

Norway lobsters mate at night. The male approaches the soft female from the rear and strokes her gently with his feelers for up to twenty minutes. Then he carefully straddles her and turns her over on her back so that their bellies are opposed. He feels around with his hollow pleopods and when he has pushed his foot inside her door, he ejaculates a spermatophore into his "trouser leg" and transfers the package with a flick or two of his tail. The act of penetration takes less than five seconds. By the time her body coating is as hard as her lover's, her "navels" will be full of gelatinous sperm parcels. How the sperms reach the eggs is something of a mystery, but it is possible that a passage temporarily opens up between holding compartment and oviduct to guide the sperms to where they are needed.

Crabs copulate in similar fashion. A sexy male will even seize a hard ripe female and carry her around in his pinchers until her armor splits. Once she's soft and malleable, they copulate face to face. He is equipped with a hollow mating leg into which he ejaculates a spermatophore. The mass of sperm is then squeezed into the female's storage space by the ramming effect of the second pair of mating legs which fit inside the first pair like the piston of a bicycle pump. Unlike the Norway lobster, who takes his sex briefly, crabs stay in a sexual clinch for anything up to five hours.

Around the edges of ponds and streams, dragon- and damselflies mate in a unique way, although their technique is somehow reminiscent of their distant crustacean cousins. The genitalia of all insects are where you expect to find them—at the tips of the long slender abdomens. But a male damselfly never experiences the satisfaction of getting his end together with his mate's. He literally does his own thing. He is equipped with a pair of sperm reservoirs situated underneath his belly, just behind the point where the legs join the body. Like the female lobster's cubbyhole, these flasks are depressions in the fly's armor. When faced with a willing female the excited male must first mate with himself. Curling his abdomen beneath him he ejaculates his spermatophores into his own reservoirs: only then is he primed for his damsel. Sidling backward toward her, he seizes her around the neck with the clasper at the rear tip of his body, so that they are in tandem—tail to head, with the male in front. The damsel retrieves her mate's spermatophore by bringing her long abdomen right around, almost in a circle, so that her vagina links up with the sperm reservoirs. Some dragonflies do all this in the air, and couples fly around in "mating rings." The sequence seems complicated, but the tandem technique of coupling may help the female to deposit eggs on or near the surface of the water, using the linked power of the male at the front to help her maneuver up and down. Since he has to use his backside for pulling the female along by her neck, the male had to find an intermediary holding area for his spermatophore.

Other insects are more straightforward, although the linking mechanisms which enable sperm packets to be transferred vary enormously. Take grasshoppers and locusts, for instance. Here consenting insects must be literally love-matched, because the approaches to the female's private parts are well guarded by horny shutters, valves, and flaps, and only the male of her species has the right key to open her up. The male locust's rump end is precisely engineered to latch onto his mate so that his penis can penetrate her soft vaginal channel and deliver

a fully wrapped present of sperms. He has a pair of rods (*cerci*) projecting from his rear, which help him get a grip on her scaly abdomen. But his chief grappling tools are two pairs of hooks at the root of his crooked penis that are spaced and shaped so that they lock onto one of the female's baseplates.

When a male locust gets the come-on, he climbs onto the back of his female and, embracing her with the front four of his six legs, lowers his abdomen so that the tip droops beneath the end of his partner's. If fertile she lets her genital guard down by opening her rear shutters and exposing her tiny sex target. Meanwhile, the male's long tubular heart, pounding in his back, has pumped up his blood pressure sufficiently to extrude his complex penis. The hooks engage beneath the female's armored abdomen, while the tip of the penis homes in on the vagina and locks into the channel which leads to the sperm-holding compartment or spermatheca. It is now apparent why the male locust has a kinky penis: the organ must double back on itself in order to dock with the vaginal orifice. While coupled, the female appears to be quite unconcerned, dragging the male around by his erection. She carries on feeding—as well she might do, because she may be linked to her lover for nearly three days; she can hardly live on love for that length of time, particularly with a load of eggs inside her that need nourishing. Sperm transmission takes much less time, but the male needs several hours to package his sex cells and, with the help of his penis, guide the parcel into his mate. It is a very elaborate bundle of fun, which is why mating is so lengthy in locustlike insects.

The spermatophore of a locust is nearly the length of our little finger. Shortly after the beginning of mating, glands in the male's reproductive system start to secrete a viscous fluid that forms the basis of the spermatophore tube. With the help of muscle power, the thin tube is slowly extruded through the penis and worms its way through the somewhat tortuous passage leading to the female's sperm-storage tank. The sperms are fed into the spermatophore tube and the base fashioned into a bladder—the ejaculatory sac—which remains implanted in part of the male's genital tract. Pressure on the sac squeezes the wriggling contents to the far end of the package buried inside the female's body.

The sperm packets made by chirping crickets are even more remarkable. Each male encloses a globule of semen inside a mass of protein, forming a pear-shaped bag with a tail. During copulation, the penis plants the tail inside the female. The innermost layer of the container is called a pressure body: as soon as the spermatophore comes into contact with the fluids in the female's system, the pressure body slowly swells, pressing on the cavity where the semen is stored and forcing it out through the tail into the female's spermatheca.

Female crickets hungry for sex have a keen appetite for the food of love. Sperm packets are full of nourishment, and if given a chance a female cricket is more likely to swoon over the calories it contains than the spermatozoa. After the crickets have parted, the female is usually left with the spermatophore bulb hanging from her rear, and she is capable of removing the whole structure with her legs and making a meal of it before the sperms have been emptied into her. From the breeding point of view, this is highly undesirable, and so male crickets have evolved various solutions to keeping the female's mind off the job until the vital process of sperm discharge has been completed.

The male tree cricket *Oecanthus fasciatus* entertains his mate to a milky meal both before and after copulation. Throughout the whole affair, he secretes the stuff from a gland on his back and so lures his mistress to mount him—crickets mate with the female riding on top, enabling the male to plug his mating tools into her from below and behind. After giving her his sperm parcel, he keeps her attention by continuing to ply her with an irresistible love potion. While she licks him all over his middle, her sperm tanks are force-filled by the action of the pressure body in his spermatophore. The male wood cricket has developed a similar strategy, but instead has the female licking at his feet, because he offers her a tempting decoy produced by a pair of spines on his hind legs.

To us, insects appear to come from an emotionless science-fiction world. No smile of satisfaction crosses the face of a cricket when he spots his chirping bride—no flush of emotion lights her up when she receives her lover's wrapped gift of sperms. But despite their cool life-style, insects have been nothing if not enterprising in their approach to mating. There are about one million different kinds of insects on our planet, and a survey of their sexual antics and tools would fill a shelf of worthy volumes.

Take the tiny fruit flies, for example, those scientifically known as *Drosophilia* (meaning "dew-loving," because of their preference for feeding on fermenting plant juices). You need a powerful lens to watch their coupling routines, but members of this large family use so many methods and positions that a fruit-fly mating manual would make the *Kama Sutra* and *The Perfumed Garden* together look like school primers. The graceful mayflies mate in midair; grotesque and wingless hunchback wasps have long-reaching sexual parts for deflowering virgin females unseen through the walls of their bridal chambers deep inside fig galls. Male bedbugs have penises like needles and make love by really getting under the mate's skin, hypodermically injecting sperm directly into the bloodstream—a method reminiscent of that of Peripatus and some marine mollusks. But no kind of insect can rival the flea. Miriam Rothschild, the world's outstanding authority on fleas, writes that the copulatory apparatus of the male flea is the most elaborate genital organ in the animal kingdom. Any engineer looking objectively at such a fantastically impractical apparatus would bet heavily against its operational success. The astonishing fact is that it works.

The rabbit flea that Miss Rothschild studied has an amazing sex life. Fleas of both sexes can live happily together on the ears of a rabbit, but they will not leap for love until their *host* gets an itch for sex. The reason is simple: to ensure the survival of her children, and so that of the next generation, the female flea must lay her eggs in the nest of a doe rabbit when she herself has a litter. The flea's breeding cycle has therefore to be synchronized with that of the host. The flea achieves its accurate timing by gearing its sex drive to the fluctuating rhythm of the doe rabbit's reproductive hormones. Only those plugged into her bloodstream stand any chance of being sexually aroused, and their chances jump as soon as a buck rabbit sets eyes on her. As the rabbit mates, her ears become flushed with blood and much warmer than usual. The rabbit fleas become feverishly active and spring back and forth between the lovers; but the doe's blood soon contains high concentrations of sex hormones, and once the fleas get a taste of them they forget the buck and cling tight to her. She therefore accumulates a heavy load of parasites at the expense of her lover, and the fleas stay on her until she gives birth. After that, her hormonal changes cause the fleas to move out in force and settle on the babies, where the fleas themselves copulate.

After feeding on young rabbit blood, perhaps containing growth hormones, the male and female fleas are suddenly made aware of each other and set off in search of sex of their own. Male fleas are by far the smaller and perhaps the weaker sex. When ready to mate, the male zigzags toward his better half and, leaping in between her legs, heaves her onto his back. Mustering all his strength, he grips her from beneath with his erect club-shaped antennae and from behind by locking his genital clasping organs into her rump. These are so bedecked with terrifying spines, struts, and hooks that it is little wonder he often seriously injures his bucking female during their twenty-to-thirty-minute period of intercourse. Once firmly in position, the male puts his astonishingly complex tool into operation.

It is only fair to report that no one quite knows the full story of how the flea's genital equipment works. The design is so involved that an American zoologist who spent a long time studying it could only report despairingly that "the thing does not make sense." The flea has a respectable penis, but the puzzle is why it has become redundant as an intromittent organ. Unlike those of most other insects, it is not erectable and is permanently hidden inside the male's posterior. He adequately makes up for this apparently useless organ by sporting another weapon, a double-barreled one in the form of two penis rods lying side by side. During copulation the two rods slide out from the male's rump and apparently uncurl like watchsprings. The female gets the benefit of both barrels. The thicker one seems to enter her first, locking into a special compartment well inside her meandering genital tract and serving to guide the smaller rod, which penetrates even farther. The operation of transferring bundles of sperm is no less involved. Using Miriam Rothschild's description, the sperm is wound around the terminal portion of the thinner of the two penis rods rather like spaghetti on the end of a fork. This rod runs through a slot in the spoonlike end of the thicker penis rod like a rope running over a pulley. The thick rod enters the female's *bursa copulatrix,* into which it fits snugly, and guides the thinner rod into the threadlike duct leading to her sperm-storage organ. The method by which the rod packs sperms in the spermatheca through this duct is not known.

As the flea faces only the simple standard problem, that of impregnating a mating partner, its solution seems to be unnecessarily complicated. Most male insects achieve good results with a single erected penis, yet fleas appear to have gone back to the drawing board and come up with a novel set of mating rods to poke around inside the female. Just how the whole apparatus evolved—and why—remains an enigma.

By our standards, there are plenty of insects with "perverse" mating habits. The males of a bee called *Centris pallida* that lives in the American deserts are in such a hurry to mate that they go digging for it. The bee grubs pupate in the ground, but the males hatch first, tunnel their way out, fighting fit and eager—then find there are no females flying around. The drone bee's response is therefore to set out in the fresh early morning air and cruise at a height of a few inches until he gets a whiff of female scent rising from the ground. The aroma bowls him over in his flight path, and he drops from the sky, groveling in the soil where the smell is strongest. Hurling back the loose rubble with his forelegs, he struggles downward to unearth a newly emerged virgin bee working her innocent course up into the world. Without a moment to lose, he grabs her and carries her off to the nearest bush.

Male bees are not the only insects to give their mates a helping hand in the furtherance of sex-all-the-sooner. The males of *Opifex fuscus,* a mosquito from New Zealand, carry around a set of tweezers on their posteriors which they use like a pair of obstetrician's forceps. Defying death by drowning, they stand around on pools and puddles attending the pupal cases hanging below the surface film. Most male mosquitos are patient enough to wait for their mistresses to emerge from their infant gowns, unfurl their glassy wings, and stretch out their six long elegant legs before tackling their private parts. Not *Opifex fuscus*; the males act as midwives to the pupal cases, splitting them open with their built-in forceps to expose the fully formed but crumpled females, and promptly copulate with them in situ.

A relative of the gipsy moth, *Orygia splendida,* takes the prize for perverse mating behavior; seen in human terms, the antics of the male smack of sex with infants. He is a normal-looking moth, with two pairs of pretty wings, but his mate is far from splendid. In a sense she never grows up, because she becomes fertile as a grub, still imprisoned in her cocoon. Without ever emerging into the light of day, she attracts the male to her by means of a gorgeous smell. When the right male is waiting outside, his exciting body-odor causes her to claw a hole in her cocoon to let him in to make love to her inside her cupboard. Afterward he flies off to find another moth Lolita, while she lays her eggs and dies without setting foot outside.

Bizarre though these sexual habits might appear, they are just the results of the competition among males to find mates and copulate with them as soon as possible. The evolution of natural eagerness means that males not only make passes but also never pass up an opportunity to copulate. A supereager male who forces his attention on a fertile female before she's even had time to hatch will outdistance his rivals at the post, and so his genes—and therefore his sexy habits—

are passed into the next generation, at the expense of slower competitors.

Some kinds of mites have thus evolved not merely precocious sex habits but also incest of a particularly dedicated nature. Variety is certainly the spice and essence of the mite's sex life. Along with the ticks, these parasitic animals are not insects but are related to the spiders. Some mites are true copulators, some have accessory penises, others mate with their feet rather like crustaceans. Ticks have no sexual tools at all, but still cope—and fearsomely. When a male comes across a female with her head firmly buried in her host and her body bloated with blood, he gets down to a bit of mouth music. Placing his proboscis firmly in her genital canal, he sets about enlarging. Once her little hole is wide enough he spins around, puts his spermatophore in the opening and pushes it up with his legs and mouth parts. Lovemaking can be fierce in mites as well, the males of some species having a pair of monstrous clasping legs to trap the female during mating. In the case of a mite that lives and loves in the soft gentle down of barn owls, the male's strong-arm tactics permanently bend the mate's body. These symbols of male virility only develop to the full if the males manage to go through the motions of mating before they are mature, however. Infant male mites who miss out pay a high price for their celibacy, remaining stunted.

Male moth mites—*Pyemotes herfsi*—take no chances, performing a double act as both midwives and lovers at their sisters' births. The females live as parasites on the caterpillars of small moths, and like many of their profession produce their young ready-formed. Newborn male mites have no desire to leave home, but hang onto their mother's apron-strings—so to speak—even piercing her flesh for nourishing body fluids. It is not laziness or sentiment that keeps them: they wait to lavish a little brotherly love on their sisters. Emerging males are treated with complete indifference, but when the head of a female peers from the mother's birth canal, her older brothers spring into action. The male quickest off the mark sets to work assisting her birth by levering with his hind legs until she is finally free enough to be pulled clear of mother. Then it is first come, first served, and the newly minted mite loses her virginity to one of her brothers almost before her feet have touched the ground. Admittedly, the females do not have much time to waste, for within a couple of days they must find a new caterpillar host, and the sooner they mate the better.

But even this does not exhaust the mite's inventiveness when it comes to mating strategies. In one kind of mite, the rivalry between males for their sisters' sexual favors has taken the action back farther into the nursery. Until quite recently this mite seemed an unpromising candidate for any sexual honor, because males were conspicuous by their absence. The females seemed to be condemned to a life of enforced celibacy, reproducing without the necessity of intercourse. The chance discovery of an aborted male made scientists search thoroughly for more and encouraged them to take a deeper look at what was going on in the wombs of pregnant females. What they found was amazing: for these mites, sex is kept tight inside the family! Far from being deprived of masculine company, by the time the females are launched into the world they have clocked up sufficient prenatal intimacy to last a lifetime. Yet their brothers are not to brave the world outside. Their adventures are limited to exploring the nether ends of their sisters' bodies, which they do in comfort: they resist being born and live incestuously inside the uterus. After all, why should they wait around outside in the cold to pick up their sisters when they can service them safely inside their mother as each passes down her production line? Distasteful though prenatal sex may seem, it is an elegant result of the male mite's urgency to be the first to impregnate his sisters and so leave the oppositon behind.

Snails and slugs, on the other hand, take their time. Terrestrial snails pass on their sperms in horny envelopes, being well advanced in the technique of packaged sex but with a few tricks of their own. *Every* snail makes sperm packages and also has a slippery little female orifice, because these mollusks are hermaphrodites. Sporting both male and female organs, each snail seems set to lead a thrilling life as the complete lover; but down in the cabbage patch, self-service is applied only to food, not sex. The snails' love life is governed by the

mathematical principle that two into two will go. When a snail feels a tingle in its penis and an empty longing in its vagina, it glides out beneath the star-spangled canopy of the night sky to find a friend in a similar frame of mind.

Before the two-way mating can take place, the two must get on the right side of each other—for a purely anatomical reason. Much of the snail's body is always housed safely inside its shell, and to be so firmly clothed is not a promising start for a lover of any kind. The garden snail has overcome this frustration by having its genital equipment relocated to open where you would expect to find the right earhole—just below and behind the right eyestalk or "horn." Before being able to cross-copulate, snails must line up their erogenous zones, and they accomplish this by necking at snail's pace. Prospective partners meet after a full frontal approach, examine the right-hand sides of each other's bodies and then proceed to chase each other's tails, sidling round and round in a slimy snail smooch. After a few turns the amorous mollusks have slipped into mating position, neck to neck, exposing their increasingly tumescent sexual targets.

The signal to get stuck into each other comes with a touch of sado-masochism. Each snail carries a calcareous lance about one-third of an inch long in its vaginal pouch and uses it like an arrow from Cupid's bow. When a snail has had enough of the hors d'oeuvre of courtship and wishes to start the main course, it stabs its love lance broadside into the naked flank of its mate. The partner quivers under the impact and, if sufficiently worked up, lets loose its own lance into the flesh of its mate. Perhaps the barbed weapons help to bind the slippery couple together while their genital organs seek out their respective targets; once both the snails have delivered their stimulant, their greatly tumescent penises penetrate each other's vaginas and they remain coupled for more than twelve hours while the spermatophores are exchanged.

Slug sex is similar to that of snails, although a few kinds mate in real style. In some species the courting couples appear to prefer copulating in comfort, making a mucus bed or cocoon and then mating beneath the sheets of slime. The copious sticky secretion may afford the lovers extra protection from predators while they are wrapped up in each other. Perhaps for the same reason, leopard slugs from Australia have specialized in suspended sex. These couples make their assignations up in the branches of bushes and shrubs. After a slow love chase, they start weaving mucus threads which they anchor at one end to a twig or leaf. Then, slipping into space, they descend on their intertwining love lines, spinning ever closer together like trapeze performers, until they finally make contact and consummate their sex act swinging in midair.

Other strange mating arrangements are found in the snail family. There is evidence that the large black slugs that occasionally plague gardeners are sometimes able to inseminate themselves; self-fertilization is certainly the rule in some marine snails. On the other hand sea hares, which look like big greenish-brown slugs, go in for group sex, the participants forming copulatory chains. Each animal acts as a male to the one in front and as a female to the one behind. In high-tide pools lurks a marine snail rejoicing in the name of *Actaeonia cocksi,* with that rather unpleasant habit already noted in the bedbug: its penis bears a nasty hollow spine which is plunged through the mate's body wall, so transferring sperm by hypodermic injection.

Some snails have even taken up the parasitic way of life. A species called *Entoconcha* lives with its head plugged into the blood vessels of sea cucumbers. It hardly resembles a snail at all, but looks like a worm three or four inches long, most of its bulk being merely an ovary and egg sac inside which reside twenty dwarf males, each virtually reduced to tiny testes.

The most advanced members of the molluskan family, the squids and octopuses, have evolved an elaborate form of packaged sex. Squids are efficient midwater interceptors powered by water-jet propulsion and capable of fast bursts of speed. Each has a well-defined head and peeps at the world through eyes every bit as keen as our own. They seem to show an intelligent awareness of what is going on, made possible by a respectable "brain." Circling their mouth they have a "mustache" of supple arms, or tentacles, to clutch their prey and investigate their surroundings. In their mating technique, squids and their allies are unique in the wild world of sex. During the climax of their act, the amorous males of some species push explosive charges of sperm in front of their lovers' faces, accomplishing this by fancy fingerwork.

Squids in breeding fettle gather together in great numbers. Unlike most of their snail relatives they come in the familiar two sexes. The blushing red males are nothing if not flexible in the way they take on a mate, and every female is ready for all possibilities, with alternative sites for the reception and storage of sperm parcels. During a full frontal pass, when a courting couple collide head-on and get their tentacles in a tangle, the male's target is a deep dimple in the middle of the female's rosette of tentacles—just below her parrotlike beak. His penis, slung beneath his stomach, is a totally inadequate tool for making love to his partner's face, and the job of transferring the packages is taken over by one of his tentacles. When sufficiently excited, he ejects a batch of spermatophores into the palm of his bottom left "hand" and thrusts them toward her "chin," an action resembling that of a guy who in the middle of a steamy embrace plunges his hand into his pants and brings out a bunch of bananas.

However, the male squid's gifts behave less like erotic food parcels than like exploding cigars; his torpedo-shaped spermatophores burst when presented to his mate. They are elaborately constructed to discharge at arm's length. The sperm bombs of the common squid *Loligo* are about 16 mm long, and a male can manufacture a dozen each day. They accumulate in a special pouch in his reproductive tract, and a large male can enter a squid orgy with an arsenal of up to 400. Each is basically a tube enclosing an inner wrapper containing a dense mass of sperm. There is also a blob of sticky glue, and a springlike filament which keeps the whole package under tension. The outer tube terminates in a detachable cap. As the spermatophore is pulled from the male's genital duct, the lid is loosened, and the internal "spring" dislodged. This primes the package, so that by the time it reaches the female the elastic contraction of the outer capsule causes the contents to eject through the top with some force. If the male moves his arm in the right direction, the sperm masses are ejaculated into the female's glandular chin cavity and securely fixed there by the cement bodies that are forced out of the containers first.

The second method of squid insemination is even more bizarre. A male squid simply pokes his sperm parcels right up his mate's nose. Just beneath a squid's head is a funnel that leads into a large cavity— rather like the space enclosed between the front of a jacket and the stomach. This contains the genital openings and gills, and the squid maintains a constant flow of fresh water through the cavity in order to respire. A male bent upon making a nasal entrance swims side by side with his partner. Embracing her head with his tentacles, his mating tool sweeps up a bunch of cocked spermatophores and, going in through her funnel, holds them for a few seconds in the region of her oviduct while they discharge. The contents simply stick around inside, sometimes even on her gills, until the eggs are shed. Fertilization is external.

Manual dexterity is not the key to the male squid's sexual success, because his mating arm, the *hectocotylus* arm, is modified for handling sperm parcels. The hectocotylus of the common squid is not very different from a normal tentacle, but in some species it lacks suckers and instead has a glandular adhesive membrane.

Octopods have highly complicated mating equipment, fashioned out of the third arm on the right. The tip is shaped like a spoon and connected to the base of the arm by a fold which acts as a sperm funnel. A male octopus prepares his mate for intimacy by gingerly touching her at arm's length. After caressing her with his mating tool he copulates by slipping the end into her mantle cavity and shooting the sex packets down the groove so that they emerge at the mouth of her egg duct.

Most people visualize octopuses as sinister giants lurking in satanic caverns on the sea bed, seizing every opportunity to drag swimmers into their deadly embrace. There are such nightmarish monsters, but most octopods are much smaller and some, like *Ocythöe*, could even grace the dreams of little children. *Ocythöe* belongs to the family of argonauts which spend their lives pulsating in the plankton, almost like jellyfish. When fully grown the female *Ocythöe* spans a foot, but her mate is a mere dwarf who lives in a "bubble." Hardly two inches broad, he stows himself away inside the transparent shells of sea tunicates after he has disposed of the contents. Despite his diminutive proportions, in the sex game he has the whip hand over his mistress, because his mating armament is extraordinarily well developed. It is by far the longest of his eight arms, its tip drawn out into a fine filament which remains coiled inside a pouch until his sex drive is aroused. He must not indulge in reckless sexual flings, but saves himself for the real thing, because he only has one stab at making love. When the sexes meet, the male draws his sex-hand out of his pocket, and, clutching his spermatophores, uses his long reach to push them through his mate's nose funnel into her body cavity. The tool then detaches, leaving him to swim away emasculated. For some time his broken sex arm continues to lash around inside the female.

The presence of these strange wriggling things was not always associated with octopod sex. Aristotle was familiar with the curious sexual habits of squids and even likened the actions of their specially constructed arms to those of penises, but he was not aware of detachable ones. Nor was the distinguished French scientist Baron Cuvier more than 2000 years later. He examined the threadlike creatures bearing suckers that hung around the egg ducts of female argonauts and agreed with the widely held view of the time that they were parasitic worms. He even christened them *Hectocotylus octopodis.* Then in 1845 a Swiss scientist, Albert Kölliker, moved nearer the facts, declaring that these *Hectocotylus* worms were no less than dwarf lovers, themselves boarding inside their relatively huge mates. Letting his imagination run riot, he even described the male's anatomy with blood vessels, gut, and respiratory apparatus. In these details he was wrong. The real truth about the argonaut (or paper nautilus) is even more startling and was stumbled upon in 1853 by Heinrich Müller, who caught some males of the species in the Straits of Messina.

It is no wonder that male argonauts avoided detection for so long. Though the female is a foot long, with a paperlike shell, the male is a midget of barely half an inch. Far from resembling a worm, he looks like a respectable short-legged octopus but carries an enormous bump on his head. This is where he stores his mighty mating arm, by far the biggest organ in his body. Despite this symbol of molluskan virility, the male argonaut is no greater romancer—indeed he is offhand with his mate, disarmed by the prospect of sex with her. He copulates by proxy, using a method reminiscent of some bristleworms. As the male matures, sperm packages are loaded into his special armpit, and when a female is nearby the arm bursts out of the envelope. Then, as if in the realms of fantasy, the unwound hectocotylus breaks free of the small male and undulates away through the sea to make contact with her. The whip end and fifty or so suckers bedecking the mating arm help it to cling to her body long enough for the escaping sperms to fertilize the eggs in her papery perambulator. What Cuvier and Kölliker had seen on the female argonaut were of course independent mating arms from males, not parasitic worms; but the name *hectocotylus* coined for them has stuck.

By our standards, the manner in which these marine creatures play the mating game is strange indeed. Not that comparisons between men and mollusks are useful, as we are such different kinds of creatures. Yet the sexual strategies of mollusks, with their parcels, love darts, and mating arms, have proved to be reasonable alternatives to our own methods of lovemaking. As a group these animals are hugely successful, both on land and in water, and have been for a very long time. It is even possible that in the distant past, when our ancestors still sported the wet look and mated in bogs and riverbeds, they too were exponents of the art of packaged sex. Evidence comes from amphibious newts and salamanders.

Although newts spend much of their lives stalking worms and insects in dry places, they retreat into ponds and ditches to breed. Their subaqueous sexual habits bear an uncanny resemblance to those of scorpions, with one major difference—the sexes meet but barely touch each other. The lovelorn male seeking to transfer the spermatophore beckons the female with an erotic scent and caresses her body with rippling water.

In spring a male newt is a handsome fellow, displaying a flashy pattern of dark blotches and a high jagged crest on his back to make him look tall. He tries to show off his decorations to every female he manages to sniff out by placing himself broadside across her bows. If his potential mate is impressed she will stay while he goes through an orderly and complicated water-courtship routine, wafting scent from his skin and cloacal glands into her face by quivering his tail.* Keeping up the steady stream of scented water, the male crawls slowly forward, followed by his interested female. When she catches him up, she bumps into his flickering tail; that is the signal for him to brake. Lengthening and lifting his tail, he drops his elongated white sperm mass, mounted on a blob of jelly. He does not react to it. Nor does she, though the fate of that capsule is crucial. Instead, he creeps forward a pace or two, then again blocks her progress in order to maneuver her blindly over the dropping zone. If the female's cloaca is nicely swollen and extended and she manages to brush against the sperm parcel, she scoops it up and draws it into her sexual tract. On average, rather less than half (43 percent) of the encounters end with the sperm package tucked neatly inside her. However, practice makes perfect, and on their third attempt, nearly two couples out of three score cloacal hits. At the end of each sex sequence the newts usually have to surface for a breather because, like us, they need air.

The touch-me-not sex of European newts is an elegant enough maneuver between couples. North American spotted salamanders indulge in an orgy of frenzied group sex in forest ponds. Forty or fifty individuals writhe together, becoming ever more excited, the surface of the water churned as though at boiling point—and the males set down their spermatophores in small heaps regardless of whether a taker swims nearby.

When frogs and toads are happy merely to couple and spawn, one wonders why newts with essentially the same life-style have gone in for internal fertilization by way of packaged sperm. Spermatozoa, tolerant of sea water, are not too keen on the sweet-water life, and so wrapping them up in an envelope of some kind could be of value

* The cloaca, found in fish, amphibians, birds, and reptiles, is not only the sexual opening. It is also the shared rear exit for gut and kidneys.

to freshwater lovers. And yet frogs and a host of fish do cope perfectly well by spilling their sex cells straight into the water. Running water may be the clue. Many newts and salamanders breed in fast-flowing streams, which would tend to wash away the sperms from where they are required. A neat system of sperm transference and internal fertilization solves that problem—and the female can go about her business of egg-laying without a male hanging around her neck.

European fire salamanders have modified this sex style with a little bodily contact so that they can perform it on land. Violently patterned in black and yellow, these salamanders have poisonous skins as a form of self-protection, but this does not prevent them from cuddling each other closely. After a male sets down his sperm packet, he wrestles his mate's pelvis into position so that she can suck it up through her cloacal lips. Many species use strong-arm tactics, having especially muscular forelimbs to embrace their squirming mating partners. Male mountain salamanders, on the other hand, get their leg over during mating, being equipped with spiny pads and spurs to keep them astride their females' backs. They enjoy a kind of cool-blooded intercourse, the male inserting his sperm packet directly into the female by wrapping his rear end around her waist. He has no penis; instead, the tumescent lips of their genital apertures come together to assist the transfer. The transaction is sealed by a cloacal kiss.

Salamanders are clearly on the verge of discovering the next best thing—the penetrating power of the penis.

6
Penis Power

The penis is crucial to our intimate style of sex. Although we men have custody of it, the phallus is an organ for both players in the mating game. Fitting snugly into the vaginal barrel, it binds human lovers together during intercourse. And, in giving and receiving pleasure, it functions for mutual delight and satisfaction.

Pleasure was not originally the purpose of the penis. Far from being a sensuous tool, it was a weapon that helped our reptilian ancestors defeat the problems of breeding high and dry. They invented the hard-shelled egg, which encapsulated the embryo in its own private puddle until it was old enough to hatch. The eggs, however, had to be fertilized before each became sealed and wrapped. So the sperms had to rendezvous with the naked ova high up in the female's reproductive tract. To assist them, the males developed a nozzle with power to penetrate and pipe their sperms into the vents of their cold-blooded mates. This "invention" enabled reptiles to graduate to the status of land lovers. It was a neat solution to the problem of achieving internal fertilization, and we can be grateful that our ancestors trod this course.

Most advanced animals have evolved ways and means of positively guiding their sperms along the right road to the female's sex cells. As we have already seen, some (e.g., insects and mollusks) which pre-package their sperms post their capsules with the help of tumescent or protruding sexual organs.

The jack-in-the-box penis sited between the legs of men and our furry relatives is only one of an astonishing array of devices for solving the problem of how to inject one's mate with a lover's cocktail. Of all animals, spiders probably have the strangest sexual procedure— copulating with their fists! If spiders could be taken back to the drawing board, the mating apparatus of the male would surely be redesigned, because operationally it seems unnecessarily compli- cated. Nevertheless, so far as the male spider himself is concerned, his tools and unique technique may suit him perfectly, because he has sex in no less than three stages.

On either side of their terrifying jaws, spiders are equipped with a pair of feelers or palps, and the tips of those brandished by the male are greatly swollen, rather like boxing gloves. Their role is not to knock the female around, but to insert and squirt semen into her genital opening; the palps are designed rather like fountain-pen fillers, each of which can draw up and release fluid at the squeeze of a bulb. Before the male takes his love life in his hands and goes courting, he first has to fill his fists with semen—a process called sperm induction. To do this, the lovelorn spider spins himself a tiny silken hammock or net the purpose of which is to catch droplets of semen as they exude from sexual pores beneath his abdomen. Afterward the male spider dips the open ends of his accessory copulatory organs into the pool of ejaculated fluid, and by the sucking action of the built-in bulbs draws it into the hollow receptacles. Occasionally sperm induction is a long-drawn-out business, and for the hand-sized tropical bird- eating spiders may take up to four hours. Then the male's troubles really begin, because female spiders must be wooed and cajoled into letting their suitors plunge their fists alternately into their bellies.

The course of true love for a male spider is paved with danger. A lot of the difficulties stem from the fact that he must court and copulate on the web his mate uses to catch prey, so although he views her as desirably dishy, she may well see him as a desirable dish. The elaborate courtship etiquette that all male spiders display is essential to the satisfactory completion of the mission, because it dulls the female's drive to kill, giving the male time to clamber on or beneath her and discharge one or both of his loaded hand-weapons into her abdomen. If successful, the male is amply rewarded; some may spend nearly half a day gently pummeling their passive partner's underside.

Male spiders use all kinds of courtship codes to woo and soothe their ferocious mates. Hunting and jumping spiders are the roaming kind and have good vision for stalking their prey in grass. The sexually primed males stand before the females and dazzle them with a precisely executed routine of semaphore signals, made all the more impressive by their conspicuously patterned front limbs. In contrast, most species that live on tacky webs strung across insect flightlines are short-sighted but have a keen sense of vibration. In many of these, the males behave like roving minstrels; they strum sweet music on their webs, which the female perceives through her feet. One technique is for the nervous male, who is often smaller than his bride, to attach a silken line to her web; this doubles as both love line and life line in case the female fails to recognize his good intentions. By twanging it, he bounces her up and down, and if he has the right rhythm for the species, she will go drowsy and let him copulate with her. That is one of a number of "musical" techniques.

The male house spider is bolder. When driven by the desire for feminine company, he crawls on a female's silken sheets and identifies himself by beating a tattoo with his bulging palps. If she perceives the love message through the tips of her feet, she'll allow the visiting troubadour to sneak into her funnel and lie beside her for a little while.

The female St.-Andrew's-cross spider, whose webs can span a road and whose legs can reach across a saucer, is the usual hard-hearted spider maneater, but she has a weakness that her timid, diminutive husband exploits—she is ticklish. Risking life and his eight limbs, he tackles her by coming to rest on the opposite face of her web, cutting a small hole in it, and tickling her feet. Unfortunately the effect is short-lived, and the female St.-Andrew's-cross spider usually regains her appetite while her dwarf lover is still dipping his fists into her. Plenty of other spidermen give their bodies as well as their sperms to their brides in an ultimate act of sexual sacrifice, so that even in death they contribute to the survival of their species, indirectly providing protein for their children.

On the whole, though, males strive not to end up as honeymoon breakfasts. When wolf spiders go courting they take a food parcel, a fly wrapped in silk, which they thrust into the open jaws of their mates before diving off in search of the sexual orifices. While the female feeds with her jaws securely buried, the male safely does his thing. (Once he has filled her sperm tanks, he may even try to grab his present back.)

Male *Tetragnathas* have even larger jaws than their mates, and are more fearsomely decorated with extra spurs and teeth. Here there is comparatively little courtship. The contestants react to each other with the equivalent of a spider's snarl, jaws wide open. When they meet, the spurs on the male's jaws mesh with the female's, so that her fangs are locked and she cannot bite him. Swinging together in midair, the male inserts his palps alternately for about fifteen minutes, and afterward rapidly disengages himself by dropping to the ground. Male money spiders gag their mistresses by offering them their heads to chew on—but they don't lose them. The heads of many kinds are strangely sculptured into lobes, grooves, and turrets, and during the preliminaries to sex the male simply walks into the open jaws of the female. She strikes out, and by seizing on the projections, each of her venomous fangs comes to rest safely in a groove. All the trapped male then has to do is to stretch out his palps one at a time and plug them into her sexual parts. When he has discharged his duties he sits very still, the female loosens her grip, and the hideous lover can slip away, refill his copulatory organs, and come back again for another poke.

Some spider sex is little more than ritualized rape, in which the males spring onto their mates and take them by force. Flower spiders even practice a form of bondage. Some of these are rather pretty animals that lie in wait in flowers which they color-match to a remarkable degree. *Xysticus* belongs to the group, but is a pale fawn spider that lurks among low foliage and mates at ground level. Sex is preceded by a short scuffle. The male climbs on the female's back and looks as though he is fondling her long slim legs. In fact he skillfully weaves her a gossamer bridal veil that ties her up and at the same time anchors her securely to the ground. Once she is safely immobilized, he elevates her rear and strokes her sexual orifice. As with many spiders, each of his palps is elaborately constructed to fit the architecture of the female's aperture, rather like a lock and key. Her hole has provision for receiving a special spur on the male's tool, and after a period of touching this spur engages, aligning the organ for pumping semen into her. During two to three hours of copulation, the male may change "hands" as much as ten to twenty times. Once he has finished his session and scurried away into the herbage, the female slowly disentangles herself from her silken bonds.

Some of the spider's relatives have different impregnating tools. At first sight the rare tropical ricinulids resemble spiders, but are more heavily armored. To the males, sex is a walkover: their two copulatory organs are situated near the tips of the third pair of legs. Sexual savagery is more in the line of sun spiders or solifuges. These aggressive carnivorous hunters scuttle around the arid and semidesert regions of the world looking like large hairy spiders. But sun spiders have fangs of monumental proportions, their edges armed with large sharply pointed teeth for crushing the life out of crickets and lizards; a South African sun spider called *Solpuga* has been named the saber-toothed tiger of the invertebrate world. They live by their jaws, and they use them for loving as well. Fertile females swoon only over brutish males. Once leapt upon by a virile male a female plays possum and allows herself to be dragged off to a cozy pad, where she is turned on her side to expose her inadequate genital opening. It's as well that she doesn't feel too sensitive in that region, because with the help of his hunting sabers he sets about massaging it. When the slit is widened, he is ready to mate with his mouth parts. Ejaculating a drop of semen onto his deadly fangs, he uses them vigorously to rub the suspension of sperms into her, then "zips her up" by pinching the edges of her orifice together, thereby sealing the fate of his sex cells. By this time the female's patience is usually on the way to exhaustion and he bounds off at the earliest opportunity.

On the other hand, harvesters—daddy longlegs, as they are known in North America—copulate by means of a protrudable penis. Harvesters have no waist, do not spin webs, and the sexes do not appear to distrust each other. There is nothing that passes for courtship either, the sex-driven pair simply approaching each other until they are face to face. The male's tubular extension to his genital aperture engages with the corresponding part of his partner, and semen is piped directly into her. Why this cool and straightforward method of copulation has not been evolved by other "spiders" is a mystery.

Intimacy goes hand in hand with breeding on the land, but many advanced forms of aquatic creatures also copulate at the climax of their sexual acts. Most fish are spawners, but the males of some are built for injecting seminal fluid into their mates. It is, for instance, difficult to visualize sharks making love. Few human bathers seeing the tall triangular fin cutting through the water would pause to investigate the shark's belly to see whether it had a couple of rods trailing from its backside. But fins are not only the key to the shark's skill as a highly maneuverable hunter, they are also instrumental in the mating game—or shark's-fin sex.

Most of the large sharks, including the much-feared great white shark, star of sea and screen, do not lay eggs but nourish their sharklets inside their "wombs." Others, such as the spotted dogfish—a small bottom-dwelling shark which many a biology student has dissected—seal each of their eggs in an attractive purse that they snag onto seaweed. When the pups have hatched the split containers are often washed ashore and picked up by beachcombers who call them "mermaids' purses." Both are sophisticated forms of reproduction and demand a system of insemination before the eggs are sealed up;

accordingly, male sharks are equipped for the job. Both sexes have two sets of paired fins—one pair at the front and another at the rear, equivalent to our arms and legs respectively. The real pair is considerably modified in the male, because between them are located two fleshy rods which project rearward from the pelvis. It used to be thought that they were prehensile claspers which held onto the female during mating, but the truth is more fascinating: the claspers are themselves copulatory organs, but derived from the very fins from which our legs evolved. For a male shark, mating is rather like putting a foot in it.

The claspers are designed for conveying semen. Both arise from the edges of the male's cloaca and have a groove on the inside, effectively converting them into open-ended tubes. Stiffened by cartilage, they contain erectile tissue that is pumped up with blood prior to intercourse.

No one has been around to witness what happens when supersharks mate, but dogfish and other small species have been seen coupling in tanks. Ordinarily the male's claspers are neatly tucked beneath the tail, but as soon as he becomes aroused one of them swings forward ready for action. Before insertion and insemination is possible, the male has to complete a sexual turn—or two—by coiling himself amidships around his mate's "hips" so that the erected clasper is brought opposite her cloaca. In many species, the male's mating rod is armed with hooks which engage on the female's thick belly skin and help anchor the tip securely in her slippery orifice. Once wrapped around, with his grooved clasper rammed home, the male shark discharges seminal fluid and lubricating slime from his cloaca into hers—a process that may take twenty minutes. Rays and skates, which are related to sharks, have the same sexual technique of fin-poking. The males of some kinds are especially well endowed, with enormous claspers flanking their tails. There is even evidence that the giant manta rays dabble with both of their claspers during copulation—alternately thrusting in one as the other is withdrawn. Females are not always passive partners during the sexual act. Indeed, female common skates may even take the initiative, seducing their flat lovers by rubbing against their mating rods until they firm up.

Much smaller kinds of fish have also exploited the advantages of fins for sex. All aquarists will be familiar with the mating technique of tooth carps—a family that includes hardy favorites for tropical tanks like mollies, platies, swordtails, and guppies. Guppies (or millions fish, as they are also called) are so active that a well-lit aquarium containing a few couples is ideal furniture for human love nests, providing a continuously running aqueous sex show.

Unlike the mating tool of sharks and skates, that of a toothed carp is fashioned out of the anal fin—the single fin that hangs from the body just behind the cloaca. Although the female's is typically fanlike, the male's undergoes a complete change at puberty, becoming a grooved copulatory organ resembling a rapier—a *gonopodium*. This rather splendid rod often incorporates a terminal catch-and-claw mechanism to hook the female by her cloaca—and it sometimes even tears her flesh. Some of the supporting rays contain sensitive spines for feeling the mate's flank or helping to arouse the male to the point of shooting his sperm down the spout. The guppy's even includes a vascular hood.

Guppies in a tank can easily be watched at work. The males are ostentatious little rakes barely an inch long, only half the size of their modestly adorned mates. Sex forever on their minds, they fish for compliments by flaunting their brilliant colors and diaphanous fins before the females. If the flattery works, the females grant their favor. Normally the gonopodium points backward, but when a male receives a come-on from a female, he swings it forward. When erected, the hollow base of the fin is brought directly over his genital pimple so that he can ejaculate masses of sperms into the gonopodial trough. Then the mating device is twisted sideways to insert in the female's vent for a few seconds while the contents are flushed into her. The guppy has a particularly mobile member, powered by several sets of muscles, so that he can reach into a female on whichever side of him she chooses to swim.

Some toothed carps are not so flexible. As their name suggests, one-sided live-bearers have to be fussy about mating positions because the males have one-sided members—some habitually drive to the left, others to the right. The sexes are made for each other, the females coming in right- or left-hand forms, their vents partly shielded from one or other side by scales. Copulation is only possible between compatible couples—between right-handed males and left-handed females, and vice versa. The strange four-eyed fish from Central America has similar problems. Lying just beneath the surface, it is designed for getting the best view of both worlds. Its eyes are set in turrets, each partitioned in such a way that half an eye is kept open in the air for fish-eating birds while the other half scans down below for food and a bit on the side. When it comes to breeding, the sexes must choose their opposite partners carefully: a female will get no satisfaction unless her mate's erection comes from the right direction—or the left, as the case may be.

The duration of courtship in toothed carps is related to the length of the male's weapon. Those with a long reach, such as dwarf top minnows, tend to engage in sneaky sex, using their length to make copulatory contact with their mates' vents while freely moving about. Accordingly they hardly flirt at all—they don't have to. Swordtails and platies must not neglect the foreplay: with relatively small gonopodia, they have to heave to in order to copulate, and so must elicit full, if brief, cooperation from their mates. They do this by impressing them with elaborate and colorful courtship rituals.

The male swordtail characin uses deception to marshal his female into mating formation alongside him. Characins are freshwater fish, mostly living in South America and Africa, and include the piranhas— "terrors of the Amazon"—and the electrically shot tetras that glow in so many tropical aquaria. The majority breed by spawning. However, the Venezuelan swordtail characin and its close relatives have evolved internal fertilization, so that after mating the female can go off by herself to deposit her eggs on plants. The problem faced by the male is to lure her to lie beside him when she is not feeling spawny. She has the makings of a single-minded spinster and will not usually tolerate males near her, let alone probing her bottom. Over the course of evolution, the male has solved the problem by becoming a confidence trickster. Trailing from the edge of each of his gill covers is a long filament, its end expanded into a fleshy bulb. When feeling sexy, he spreads one of the gill covers and jerks the darkened bulb before the nose of the "frigid" female as though it was a tasty water flea. Programmed to be gullible, she falls for his line and nibbles at the bait. By the time she realizes she has been sold a dummy, the male's sexual appetite has been satisfied, his sperms well and truly squirted up inside her vent.

The tool of the copulating frog is yet another design, coming close to what we would all call a proper penis. Although spawning is the normal sexual style of frogs and toads, a handful of species has cultivated intimate relationships. From their name, live-bearing toads from Tanzania and Guinea would seem as likely a species as any to show us the amphibious penis. Unfortunately, the males are no better endowed than other toads, and love their mates—warts and all—by means of the genital kiss. More fertile hunting grounds are half a world away, in fast-running streams of ice water high up in the Rockies. Here the female American tailed frogs, though they lay strings of eggs like most other respectable frogs, are fertilized internally—perhaps because the rapid flow of water would disperse the sperms and render useless the orthodox style of piggyback spawning. The male's tail is his sexual survival kit for mating in torrents: he uses it to transfer sperms directly into his partner's vent. In fact this 10-mm "tail" is in no way equivalent to the muscular blade of the tadpole, but simply a fixed tubular extension of the cloaca, all ready for making a rear-entry approach between the female's slippery thighs during a mating clinch.

Lizards and snakes have gone in for one-upmanship in the mating game. Each can boast two copulatory organs—one for the right and one for the left—called *hemipenes*. A male lizard keeps his two mating weapons tucked away inside his tail rather like a two-fisted mitten; they give him a virile bulge between his hind legs. He only turns them outward during the act of copulation. Unfortunately, some lizard lovers have a problem distinguishing between the sexes. The American anoles, for instance, are all basically green for camouflage in their leafy surroundings. The males identify themselves by flashing a triangular flap of red or blue skin below their chin. If another male is flashed, he instinctively returns the signal, but a female lacks the chin flag and gives away her sex by *not* waving back. Instead, she gives him the nod, bobbing her head up and down.

Male or female African rainbow lizards are instantly identifiable. The males have coats of many brilliant colors, with orange heads, indigo-blue bodies, and multicolored tails of off-white, orange, and black. This acts like warpaint for inspiring fear: these lizards are keenly territorial, and defend their freeholds by performing pushups and chasing rivals. The females are predominantly brown and are promptly recognized for what they have to offer—the chance of sex. When one sets foot on a male's patch, he blushes bright orange and nods his approval. If she doesn't dig him or his intentions, the female rainbow obstructs his passes by waltzing around. If motivated to mate, she pauses, presents her flank to him, and lifts her tail vertically to reveal her genital slit. Male lizards are not exactly the most gentle lovers in the world; the rainbow grabs her by the scruff of the neck, cocks one of his hind legs over her back, brings his pulsating and swollen vent beneath her tail to make contact with hers, and then everts one of his hemipenes into her cloaca to complete the sexual connection. After ten seconds, the hemipenis is withdrawn and it is all over.

Other species have different methods of subduing their partners, who usually show desperate signs of wishing to escape what's in store for them. The males of many kinds of anoles quiet their females by

walking all over them, nudging and poking their necks and stroking them with their thighs. These often possess a series of glands, or femoral organs, which during the rubbing will anoint the female's body with scent which appeals to her reptilian senses. During the foreplay, the hemipenes start to swell inside the male's vent. Taking a firm grip on his partner's lower flank, he coils himself around her pelvis, tucking his tail underneath to make genital contact. The female Caroline anole lizard may feel the male thrusting away inside her for forty minutes. She will even so never get a chance to be astonished by her lover's amazing member. Nor will any other reptile, because the hemipenes only sneak out during cloacal contact.

The hemipenis is not a hollow organ, like a man's penis, but simply bears a furrow to direct the flow of semen from the male's genital duct into the female's cloaca. It plays no part in conveying kidney wastes to the exterior. Nevertheless, hemipenes are magnificent when fully everted by a passionate owner's blood pressure. Each one is bulbous, like a clenched fist; although some are smooth, most are richly ornate with lobes and folds. Iguanas have grotesque hemipenes with a curious honeycomb texture, while Teid lizards from America possess transversely ridged ones. All are different: in fact, male lizards can be identified by their hemipenis profiles. Why should some lizards have relatively simple plungers, whereas others copulate with corrugated cocks as lavishly adorned as the richest baroque architecture?

Part of the answer may lie in the time needed for the job. The males of some species take only a few seconds to copulate. Lizard lovers with such speedy mating habits—like the rainbow lizard—tend to sport fairly straightforward hemipenes that can be rapidly in and out of their mates' posteriors. Anoles that take more time are equipped with more elaborately designed hemipenes, and the transverse ridges may help hold them within the female's cloaca during protracted periods of intimacy. Snakes support this explanation, because many indulge in marathon thrashes, and the males are furnished with positively vicious-looking penises.

Snakes have no limbs with which to hold onto each other—although male boas still show off their legs as a pair of spurs for digging into and stimulating their mates. Coupling serpents simply entwine their elongated slithering bodies. There is no better place to see them in sexual huddles than in Manitoba's fantastic snake pits, where garter snakes mate en masse among the aspens. The snakes sleep away the winter months in their communal dormitories, and when the spring sunshine starts to warm up the countryside they are ready to celebrate their awakening with a super love-in on the hot rocks. Thousands of these harmless snakes emerge from the pits, the ground seething with sexing serpents. Some get knotted in bushes and hang together in copulating bunches, waving around like Medusa's locks. After a few days the orgy cools as the zapped garters gradually disperse for their summer hunting grounds in the surrounding bogs. Garters, like all snakes, depend upon the male's monumental erection to tie them in wedlock perhaps for as long as a day.

The size and shape of the hemipenes vary greatly among snakes. Some African burrowing snakes possess a pair of wormlike rods of extraordinary length, practically as long as the tail. Most have a pair of single-headed hemipenes, but vipers are astonishingly well equipped, each of their two hemipenes being as deeply forked as a snake's tongue. A male rattlesnake or copperhead is therefore the proud owner of no less than two double-barreled penises. If both could be simultaneously protruded, this venomous snake would look as though it was fitted amidships with a pair of fancy rowlocks.

The double penises are ideally constructed to catch inside the female's vent. When everted (inside out), each resembles a medieval mace. Those of rattlesnakes and adders are studded with backward-projecting spines—small ones near the tip, relatively huge ones close to the base—which inevitably bite into the female's cloacal walls during intercourse. Such decorations prevent the male's weapon from being prematurely disengaged before the female has been well and truly inseminated. But why do snakes and lizards need two sets of copulatory organs, when they seem to use only one at a time?

During mating, a reptilian lover must be "ambidextrous," as proficient in taking the plunge from the right as from the left. Since both sexes inconveniently have tails, which tend to get in the way, insertion is best achieved by a penis projecting sideways while the male coils around the female's hips. By having two "penises," the male is armed for a left- or right-flank action. If cuddling against his partner's left side, he draws his right organ and vice versa. Crocodiles and alligators manage with a single central "penis." They not only possess handsome tails but are also well along the road toward proper penis-powered intercourse—and that's where we come in, because we owe the design of ours to the fact that we are mammals.

Nothing in the animal kingdom stands up to the mammalian phallus. Unlike the mating tools of reptiles, the mammalian penis is made for both sexual intercourse and urination. Most of the time the penis is either folded, shrunken, or sheathed. It changes dramatically when there is a firm proposal of sex. Then the penis of mice or men rises to the occasion, becoming stiffened and erect. Since these organs sometimes seem to have minds of their own, men (and women) often see the penises as distinct personalities and refer to them by all sorts of names, some more endearing than others.

Penises can be divided into two fundamentally different types. The human variety is typical of the vascular club, the distinguished membership including not only those of other monkeys and apes but also those of horses, tapirs, elephants, rhinos, and whales. The vascular penis is a fleshy organ, limp when relaxed but standing up in response to a throbbing heart. Blood pressure erects and stiffens it: the shaft of the vascular penis contains columns of spongy tissue attached at one end to the pubic bones and capable of gross tumescence when gorged with blood. During sexual foreplay, or while having erotic thoughts, the arteries servicing the erectile tissue are widened and the corresponding veins are constricted, thereby bloating the barrel with blood; the action of a special muscle further strangles the venous drainage of the penis. Since the penis has to fill with blood, the acquisition of an erection powerful enough to drive into a mate takes a little time. For example, on seeing a mare a stallion may take two minutes to develop a full erection, growing from a few inches to nearly two feet in length as blood is pumped into it. Penis design therefore dictates to some extent the nature of the mating game; lovers equipped with a hydraulically operated penis need periods of stimulation before they are in full fettle.

On the other hand, males equipped with fibroelastic organs are capable of instant erections. Cud-chewing beasts like deer, antelope, sheep, and cattle possess penises like thin pokers. These instruments are always rigid, being constructed from hard gristle and not relying much on blood pressure to mobilize them. A couple of kinks along the shafts allow them to be kept folded back under tension into neat S-shaped packages beneath the male's belly. A bull is therefore always ready for a quick stab at a willing target. By simply relaxing the penis retractor muscle, his rod shoots out of the scabbard in a flash into the cow's vulva. During the brief act of copulation, the penis hardly increases in girth or length—it simply straightens out. After ejaculation, the retractor muscle withdraws it, flexing it back into shape inside the belly for protection. But not all fibroelastic penises are the same shape. The ram's, for example, terminates in a thumb-length filament known as a filiform appendage. During ejaculation it rotates rapidly like a propeller and sprays semen round the uterine opening. Nature is nothing if not resourceful, and many other mammals, like monkeys and rodents, have a fairly obvious method of ensuring that their penises do not crumple under the pressure of lovemaking—they are built around bones. Those of seals, sea lions, and walruses are the most spectacular. Every bull of these species grows a bone in its penis called a baculum. Immature males have insignificant baculums, but with the onset of sexual maturity the internal strengthening rod suddenly increases in stature. The handsome sticks of elephant seals are often sought as ruler-sized souvenirs by visitors to the waters of the deep Southern Hemisphere and Antarctica, where the belligerent

bulls have springtime crushes on the cows. Mating in elephant seals often resembles rape, because the four-ton bulls are almost double the length of their cows. The males roll their corpulent carcasses on top, setting their flab rippling to the rocking rhythm of their vigorous sexual thrusts. When in position, the bull flips his red, bone-stiffened shaft into the tip-tilted tail of the cow, and for five minutes pummels and squashes her. After seeding her, the master shuffles off, his penis safely retracted inside his rear.

These are the extremes of penis types. The individual details differ: some are more unusual than others, for instance those of many marsupials.

The first European to set eyes on a wallaby (on the southeast coast of New Guinea in 1606) saw fit to comment upon the unusual disposition of its private parts. He was the Spanish explorer Don Diego de Prado y Tovar, who had just accompanied Luis Vaez de Torres through the stormy strait that now bears his name. Making landfall much farther north, he recorded that a native animal the crew killed for the pot had a stomach full of ginger leaves, and testicles that dangled from a "nerve like a thin cord" and were located in front of the penis. He was spared further surprises. Although this was possibly the first sighting of a kind of kangaroo, it was not the first discovery of a marsupial, which happened in Brazil in 1500. A female opossum was collected and much excited the scholars of the day by her nursery pouch, in which she protected and provisioned her young with milk. There were further discoveries to be made. When a cat-sized North American opossum was cut open by the English anatomist Edward Tyson in 1698, he discovered a forked vagina leading to paired wombs. The animal was accordingly scientifically christened *Didelphis,* "two vaginas."

When that first pregnant Virginia opossum was examined nearly four centuries ago, the scientists of the day were highly intrigued as to how the cluster of helpless bee-sized babies had been conceived and come to occupy her snug pouch. Nothing of the kind had been seen before. Her unique nursery purse, situated beneath her belly rather like a kangaroo's, was taken to be a sort of exterior womb. Such a strange arrangement called for an equally unusual method of procreation. It was solemnly suggested that the female opossum produced her children in her nostrils and later transferred them to more comfortable and less congested quarters by sneezing them into her pouch. The theory was backed by observation, because just before the tiny pink young appear, female marsupials do spend some time with their noses buried in their pouches. But the significance of this behavior was misinterpreted: the mothers were not sneezing but vigorously cleaning out their chambers in preparation for receiving the almost embryonic young, which are of course conceived in the normal way for mammals and born by the usual route.

With hindsight, the first notion about how opossums generated seems absurd, but it was no more preposterous than many quaint ideas about reproduction that were accepted in those days. Our forefathers of less than ten generations ago believed that fleas spontaneously arose from filth, that mice were created in piles of old rags, and that shellfish appeared by magic from the sand on the seashore. Nevertheless it was widely accepted that, for most larger animals, procreation needs the cooperation or coupling of males and females. Even the writers of the Book of Genesis appreciated that. Although there is no mention of the pursuit of carnal pleasures in the Garden of Eden, there must have been sex in the Ark, which was conveniently populated by pairs of each species with the view to repopulating the purged world after the Flood receded.

Opossums are zoologically interesting animals because they give us an idea what the ancestors of the Australasian marsupials looked like. It is thought that a few primitive opossumlike creatures rafted across to Australia about seventy million years ago and found that they had the island continent almost to themselves. Evolution ran riot, and from humble beginnings sprang up the whole range of marsupials, including animals as different as koalas and wombats, flying phalangers and hopping kangaroos. Most inherited the opossums' strange sexual apparatus. Not only do the females have Y-shaped vaginas, but the males are blessed with penises to match. A bull kangaroo has a penis like a pitchfork: the shaft is straightforward, but the tip is divided into two prongs, which presumably during the act of mating are thrust home to engage the two horns of the cow's vagina.

Even more astonishing things happen in Australia. When the spotted native cats—or quolls—feel like it, no less than two lengthy erections sprout from between their legs like two pink probes, one on top of the other! Having the choice of two, as it were, one might think that these fierce cat-sized carnivores are either lucky or in a constant dilemma over which to use when the urge takes a grip of them. However, closer examination shows that only the lower shaft is a proper penis, and the upper one appears to be a greatly modified foreskin which, when erect, is rather less stiff than the real thing—an odd arrangement.

Graham Settle, an Australian zoologist who breeds these night-loving animals in Sydney, spent a night beneath a wire-floored cage peeping at a pair of quolls working themselves up to a routine four-hour mating session. What he saw solved the puzzle. When the female was ready to mate, her cloacal lips puffed up and gaped to reveal her vagina, but her sexual orifice was within a flea's foreskin of her back passage. In fact, they were so close together that any normally endowed mate would just as likely have gone off course and wasted his bolt in her rectum. But the male native cat is no ordinary lover, and his extra appendage is the right distance from his penis to block the female's rectal opening—which is precisely what happened when Graham Settle was on the watch. The male accomplished the seemingly impossible feat of simultaneous anal and genital intercourse. A pair of sexing quolls thus fit together like a two-pin plug and socket and only love-match one way. The male's unique anatomy has evolved to prevent the danger of sperm wastage, but as a result both male and female quolls can perform double-decker sex.

For pigs, the mating routine has some unusual twists. Sows get well and truly "screwed," the boar having a long fibroelastic implement with a unique spirally shaped tip similar to a corkscrew that bores into the cervix deep inside the vagina during sexual encounters. The boar sets about the art of porcine seduction by slobbering and breathing heavily in the sow's face. If she is ready for sex, his lusty mouth-odor strikes her rigid, with an arched back, and gives her a glazed expression in her round little eyes. The stuff that bowls her over is actually manufactured in the boar's big testes but travels around in his bloodstream to the salivary glands before finally being exuded in his copious precopulatory froth. The sow gets a noseful of his erotically scented breath when, driven by desire for each other, the courting couple nuzzle their heads together. As soon as she sniffs and swoons, the boar enters her without further ceremony.

Members of the cat family have penises as remarkable as those of pigs. When the ginger tom next door goes for a moonlight pad, he'll keep a sharp eye open for desirable pussies into which to slip his thorny mating thimble. But neither alley nor jungle cats go courting in Disneyland, where feline love affairs flourish at the stroke of a cartoonist's brush. In the real world no amount of affectionate rubbing, overtures of purring, or nicely packaged presents of mice will turn the head of a cool female cat. On the contrary. They resent males taking any sexual interest in them at all when they are not in the mood, and violently rebuff advances by fiercely spitting and striking out. Being an accomplished huntress, a she-cat can deliver a painful cuff with her paws of sharp sickles and a deadly bite with a mouthful of knives and daggers.

The males accordingly are wise enough to let her call the tune. She suddenly becomes friendly toward the toms, allowing them to lick her head and vulva. During the preparatory period she is a teaser and displays her normally out-of-bounds body to her eagerly waiting lovers by performing a floor show, sensuously rolling around and squirming a few feet from them. But there is no point in pouncing on her until she assumes the mating position in her own time. She may get the uncontrollable urge to feel a tom on her back, his prickly glans between her thighs, in the middle of a bout of rolling. In a split second she rights herself, forelegs crouched, haunches raised and tail twisted to one side to expose her vulva. That's what the audience of toms has been waiting for, because they know that her temper is now momentarily neutralized by a carnal impulse, and she's safe to mount. In a flash the nearest or dominant tom leaps on her and secures his sex kitten in a neck grip. Meanwhile the female's extended rear legs alternately tread and move rearwards, elevating her vulva to meet the male's slowly protruding clawed penis. Then, with one vigorous thrust, the tom's erection penetrates her. By her reaction it looks as though he really slips her a crippler, because she usually lets out a piercing howl, and within fifteen seconds frees herself. The tom jumps clear of his spitting mate before he receives the sharp ends of her weapons. Experience tells him that, whether she suffered pain or enjoyed masochistic pleasure from his barbed prick, she will be back for more every twenty minutes or so during her day or two of nymphomania.

Why the tomcat has these rough penile spines is something of a puzzle. One theory is that they are simply holdfast devices: since the sharp barbs are directed backward toward the base of the penis, they

should not interfere with insertion, but should impede withdrawal—
at least while the erection is strong. Or are the spines there for the
delectation of the male, providing him with enhanced thrills during
the sexual act? It took a French zoologist to see it from the female's
point of view. Her loud cry at the moment of penetration suggests a
more likely theory, that the "thorns" provide a powerful stimulus to
her genital tract. The notion made no sense until it was discovered,
in 1934, that the cat is one of a large number of species in which the
excitement of copulation triggers off the process that launches eggs
from the ovaries into the tubes where they are fertilized. North
American mole shrews, for example, are continuously in heat for
thirty-three days in the absence of a male. But once they have mated
several times, the eggs are shed within three days of the first bout of
lovemaking. Doe rabbits ovulate ten hours after insemination by a
buck. Induced ovulation—as it is called—is characteristic of a whole
range of carnivores. Cats are even more responsive, however: females
in estrus can be encouraged to deliver their eggs within twenty-four
hours by stimulating their genitalia with a glass rod. The penis of a
tomcat is probably much better built for producing the intense level
of vaginal stimulation needed to start the microscopic eggs rolling
down the oviducts, particularly since the periods of insertion are so
brief.

Although male members of the cat family possess the most vicious-
looking mating tools, many other mammals have penises adorned
with a cruel spike or two. Many a rodent, for example, has a penis
surmounted by a "thorn" for added penetrating power and stimulation. Rats need it, because they inject semen directly into their
partner's uterus. We and our primate cousins have especially smooth
members. But perhaps we too could profit from a rod like a briar stem,
or at least a knobbly one. After all, for humans the penis is not merely
a syringe for injecting semen; it is also a means for dispensing pleasure.
While the male gets his by thrusting his glans deep into his girl, she
is thrilled by the feel of the shaft rubbing against the lips of her vulva
and clitoris.

Unlike the cats but like us, the five kinds of rhinos have a vascular penis, but the tips have to be seen to be believed. Bull rhinos are the original adherents of flower power: each one sports a long erect penis capped by a gorgeous purple structure fashioned like a daffodil; from the center of the partially lobed hood projects a handsome trumpet, and that is not the end of it. Attached to the base of the glans—just behind the ''petals''—are a pair of lateral flanges or lobes (depending

upon the species) which are stiffened by blood pressure during erection.

If cow rhinos could be made to romance by being proferred a flower, then the bull's penis would make sense. Needless to say, they don't. With their backs turned against the bull while copulating, they do not even get a glimpse of his pretty penis. Nevertheless, its design may answer one of his problems. His heavy bulk astride the flanks of an amorous cow, he cannot see her sexual bull's-eye. But slowly and surely his penis gradually protrudes from its sheath way back beneath his tail and closes in on her crotch. As his love blossoms, the penis starts to move around; the lobes and trumpet weave of their own accord and feel for her vulva. Once the tip engages with the correct orifice, the remainder of the penis—lobes, flanges, and all—is walked in, and remains there for perhaps half an hour.

Both Indian and African elephants, too, are in the power-tool business, having to overcome the mechanical problem of linking up and plugging their private parts during their rare bouts of pachydermous passion. Like rhinos, elephants pay for being big—they are fairly rigidly constructed to support their enormous bulks. They are not great movers in the mating game, because a ten-ton bull is incapable of thrusting vigorously with his pelvis to work his penis home. He gets some assistance from the cow's design, because over the course of evolution her sexual opening has been relocated from the usual position to a site way down beneath her baggy belly where you would almost expect to find her navel. This saves the bull the impossible task of having to bring his groin close up against her thighs to copulate. He stands a better chance of reaching a low-slung slit, and can leave the energetic business of making love to his massive self-drive penis. This is a veritable power pack, containing not only erectile tissue but also its own engine of muscles for thrashing about in all directions. When fully unsheathed it is flexed, like a forward-directed meathook. Rarely still for a moment, it searches around under its own power for the cow's sexual fleshpot, and usually scores a hit after executing a series of "upper cuts" between her legs. Once nestling against her stiffened arm-length clitoris, the swollen tip is driven into her chamber by a series of pistonlike movements. After a few seconds, the up-and-down motion excites the bull to ejaculate. That's how elephants cope with their oversized love life.

Some much smaller beasts have to face up to difficulties as monumental as those of the heavyweights. To wonder how male hedgehogs come together is a stock joke. For 2000 years curious naturalists have pondered upon the uncomfortable dilemma; that is all anyone did until after the Second World War. One theory had it that a sow with the urge would turn over on to her own bed of nails, thereby allowing the boar to penetrate her while sitting astride her soft, unguarded stomach. Or did these pincushions rear up on their hind legs and couple face to face? In 1948, after having had the not altogether original idea of actually watching hedgehogs at it, H. Stieve was able to give a congress of German zoologists in Kiel the simple story.

Hedgehogs just mate carefully, with a routine designed to make the connection between the couple as painless as possible. Courtship resembles a protracted duel, with much growling and snorting, and at this stage a persistent boar can easily make the sow's hair stand on end. But after a while, she apparently gets used to his advances and her spines settle. When she is ready, she stretches out on the ground with her prickles meekly flattened. Like most respectable mammals, the boar mounts from the rear. He erects his dispropor-

tionately long penis, which can engage with her elevated hindquarters without danger of her spines tearing his groin. Apart, then, from having a long-reach penis, the hedgehog's mating habits are not unusual.

Porcupines are, if anything, even more prickly than hedgehogs, with their coats of long sharp quills that can be erected and rattled in the face of bothersome enemies. The porcupine is generous with the gifts endowed it by nature, and if pestered too persistently will leave a few of them behind, sticking painfully into the would-be predator. The North American species bristles with about 30,000 barbed spines and can further protect itself from the rear by lashing out with its spiked cudgel of a tail. A rutting male strutting behind the female has to be careful of her wagging tail.

But during their few hours of heat the females seem as anxious as the males that their turgid and enlarged genital lips should be adequately exposed. Normally, porcupines object strongly to being touched anywhere, especially around the base of their tails; they like to keep their private parts private. As the rut approaches in the fall, their inclinations change, and both sexes become increasingly keen on having their genitals touched. A sexy female may even give herself a bit of stick, holding a long twig with her forepaws like a witch rides a broomstick, and walking around erect with her vulva rubbing up against the end of it. The behavior looks like masturbation. Her mate goes through similar motions, rubbing his penis and scrotum on projections—and the greater the projection used, the greater seems his sense of satisfaction. He takes special interest in her "dildo"— or anything else that has been smeared by her musky labial lips or wetted with her smelly urine. Grasping her stick, usually in his left paw, he walks around three-legged, holding her love-object against his penis and dousing it with his urine. If he has nothing precious of hers to hold, he contents himself by reaching back toward his balls and dribbles onto his paw. Toilet water plays an important part in porcupine love affairs.

When a male American porcupine is sufficiently aroused by sniffing and rubbing noses with his mate, he gives her a standing ovation with a fully erect penis stretched out before him like a pencil. If the female is ready and ripe, she too rears up on her hind legs, faces the male, and rubs noses with him. Trappers trudging through the North American woodlands often saw porcupines embracing like this and claimed that they were kissing and mating. The trappers had it wrong, because from the standing position the male showers his mate not with kisses but with urine. After a minute or two her underside is drenched from nose to tail with her lover's spray. The female may then invite copulation by going down on all fours, raising her tail to reveal her vulva and backing into the male. Copulation takes place with the male standing up thrusting into her by flexing his bristly knees. He uses his tail like a stool and derives extra thrust from it by alternately bending and straightening it out. He needs all the help he can get, because a female porcupine's sexual urge is almost insatiable while she is in estrus. For several hours she maintains a high level of sexual aggressiveness, attempting to reestablish sexual contact almost as soon as the male dismounts. Within twenty minutes he may be called upon to mate eight times, and by the end of the session is exhausted.

The porcupine's sex life is nevertheless ploddingly unexceptional when compared with the really wild extremes of animal erotica.

7
Bondage, Buggery, and All That

If you lead a dog's life, you will find sex is a tie. Dogs have no choice in the matter, because all of them—from freely roaming wolves to pet poodles—practice an unusual kind of pair bonding.

Coupling is preceded by the ritual of canine courtship, with much panting and sniffing around the base of each other's wagging tails. During foreplay, the dog regularly excuses himself from the female's company, cocking a leg and sprinkling his scented urine around. After the initial introductions are over, the male devotes his entire attention to his partner's behind, relishing her sexual scents and lapping up her desirable genital juices. When she has been sufficiently titillated by his nuzzling and tongue play, she asks him to mount by striking a highly erotic pose, raising her rump, and twisting her tail to the side.

No experienced dog can refuse such an invitation, but one wonders whether what happens next comes as a surprise to young, naïve animals embarking on their first love affairs. Once the come-on has been accepted, there can be no going back. When Fido gets stuck into the job, he becomes just that—love-locked inside his bitch for anything up to half an hour. Both animals contribute to the tie. The dog has no ordinary penis: once erected inside the female, its posterior part swells rapidly like a balloon. Also, the bitch's vagina has a grip like a vise and closes in on the male's penis so tightly that withdrawal is temporarily impossible. Although dogs start copulating in the regular mating position, the male perched behind the female, after a minute or so he usually dismounts, makes himself more comfortable by throwing a leg over his trapped penis, and turns his back on the bitch. The two then stand like a pair of outward-facing Siamese twins joined by their bottoms. While intimately linked, there is little the couple can do except wait quietly. If the bitch tries to break away before the male has finished ejaculating, she simply tows him around backward by his erection—a highly uncomfortable frolic for his already stretched nozzle. Deflation must come as a merciful release. The wonder is that the love tie rarely results in injury. Nor does it apparently reduce the dog's appetite for more of the same treatment, because if given the chance a virile male is capable of getting himself in this sort of jam five times a day.

To us, the term *bondage* conjures up extravagant images of sexual slavery. Indeed, people who freak out on gags, chains, and padlocks deploy them to bring their partner's body under complete submission: a lover with ankles and wrists shackled to the bedposts is not going anywhere except to play the game his or her mate has in mind. The kind of "games" dogs get up to have nothing to do with sexual depravity, and they do not work up love-ties on the sidewalks for our amusement. Even affluent city hounds cannot afford to be that indulgent in their breeding business, which is far too serious. Yet the results are similar, because bondage is concerned with mating monopoly. In the bedroom, tying one partner down guarantees mating rights to the other. So it is in nature.

Bondage of some kind or other is usually in the male's interest, and for a very good reason—he can never be *quite* sure that he is fathering the female's children! Females are as capable of being promiscuous as males, and that is as true of lady weevils as of women. A male who invests a lot of time and effort courting and copulating with a female of his species will realize nothing from his investment in the currency of the life game unless his sperms alone seed her eggs. Being only human—as it were—she may have already had affairs, and her eggs may have already been fertilized by her previous lovers. Even if our male was her first love and he found her ripe, another may have mated with her soon after he had dropped exhausted from her back, and the

rival's sperms could have displaced his in the reproductive sweep-
stakes. In the best of marriages there is a degree of male anxiety about
what the wife is up to when his back is turned. Though this could be
mere male chauvinism and anxiety, it is based upon biological realism.
It may matter little to a female who fathers her offspring, providing
the male is one of the finer examples of the species; but from a lower
animal's male's point of view, female infidelity is counterproductive.
A female is only biologically useful to him if, through the sex act, she
helps to pass on *his* genes, so any trick that helps him to ensure her
faithfulness has survival value.

Brute force is the most straightforward method of gaining sole
sexual rights. The effectiveness of the big-bully beachmaster seals in
jealously guarding their harems cannot be doubted. The males of
many hoofed mammals similarly herd their cows well away from the
attentions of rivals. Bondage takes a more direct form, however, in
the lower animals. Some male crustaceans keep a mate to themselves
by the simple expedient of carrying her around for days on end. Crabs
are an example. For much of the time, the female is soft—she is likely
to mate just after molting—and so the larger male could be helping
to protect her and her load of fertilized eggs from predators as well
as from other competitors. Isopods and amphipods—shrimplike crustaceans—swim around in tandem, the more powerful males hanging
onto the ripe females by means of specialized seizing legs.

Some insects do likewise. Massive scarabs, known by such impressive names as hercules, rhinoceros, and elephant beetles, are
among the most magnificent insects alive. The six-inch-long males
are bedecked with monstrous horns and fanciful knobs but are not
subtle operators when it comes to romancing. They simply grab their
females and carry them off to secluded places, sequestered from the
opposition, until they have well and truly had their way.

The universal dilemma for males is highlighted around the warm
moist surface of cowpats where khaki-colored dung flies copulate.
The males congregate there because that is where the females deposit
their eggs. He who mates last fathers 70 per cent of the female's eggs.
When she arrives in the vicinity she is quickly grabbed, flown a few

feet away from the cowpat and inseminated. She remains lusty for sex until she has laid her clutch, so after copulating the male has a choice: to ride her until she turns frigid, but at the expense of wasting mating opportunities with other females, or to abandon her and face the danger of being cuckolded by another male, losing progeny when she consents to a second insemination. With the dung fly there is such fierce competition for females that one bird in the hand is worth two in the bush, and so natural selection has favored males who cling for a while to their brides after mating. That way, takeover bids are discouraged, though the guarding phase must cost each male many missed opportunities. Male locusts often stay mounted on their mistresses for two days after copulation. Even this pales into insignificance when compared with the "patience" of male weevils—*Rhytirrhinus surcoufi*—which have been recorded on the backs of their mates for a month without losing contact.

Such dedication resembles that of male frogs, which may cling to females for days so as not to miss the egg strings as they are shed. The males of certain narrow-mouthed toads such as the Kansas ant-eating frog and the African *Breviceps* take it easy while waiting on the female's pleasure: instead of clasping, they stick themselves to the rumps of their big fat mates with a glue secreted from their chests.

Greatly protracted copulation is another kind of bondage, keeping the female under her mate's control. Perhaps dogs are playing this ballgame. They are basically sociable animals, and a bitch in heat has magnetic appeal for all the males in the pack. Copulation is probably the prerogative of the top dog, especially when the bitch is in the hottest, most fertile phase, and the success rate of his sperms is undoubtedly improved by the enforced and lengthy period of intromission and ejaculation. Should a subordinate male take her on afterward, his sperms have a much reduced chance of fathering her pups. Many insects like moths and butterflies are regularly on the job for a day or so, a tiring way of imposing monogamy. Houseflies spend much less time in tandem, but far longer than is strictly necessary simply to transfer semen. A male needs ten to fifteen minutes to inseminate his partner, but copulation lasts for about an hour; undoubtedly the male is taking extra time to guard his reproductive investment while she is still in the mood for sex.

It would be easier and less time-consuming to seal up the female's genital orifice—which is precisely what a lot of insects and mammals do. Chastity belts were in fashion long before medieval knights invented them to guarantee the freehold of their ladies' private parts during their long crusades abroad. Such techniques were being employed, in a far more sophisticated fashion, in the countryside around their castles and manors by bees, butterflies, and mosquitos. The insects had no need of awkward contraptions of wrought iron to keep their females on the straight and narrow; they simply sealed up their rears with hard-setting seminal fluid. Temporary copulatory plugs are not confined to insects. Bats, hedgehogs, marsupials, and many rodents have them. The male rat is equipped with a special coagulating gland that mixes an enzyme called vesiculase with his semen. After he has ejaculated, the enzyme's action makes the semen set, effectively blocking the vagina. Should the plug fail to form, the female apparently does not become pregnant. It has always been assumed that the plugs functioned like bottle-stoppers, assisting insemination by holding in the sperms. Evidence from insects, however, suggests that their purpose is to prevent the females from remating and to keep rival sperms at bay, because if the gelatinous bungs are experimentally removed, fertilization seems to be unaffected. Male mosquitos leave their lovers truly stuffed up, and their viscous semen remains in situ for well over a day—just through the period when the females are still sexy enough to remate. In little dewflies—*Drosophila*—competition for ripe females is again intense, but the first male to make it with a virgin places his seal of approval firmly in her rump, and so enforces her faithfulness in body if not in mind.

From the male's point of view female butterflies most certainly cannot be trusted as they lightly flit between the flowers, intent only on sipping nectar and being seduced in the sunshine. Mating is high on the male's agenda too, and he foils any further philandering by his mates by filling the copulatory opening of each one with a pluglike structure called a sphragis. This is made by the male's accessory sexual glands—the same ones that secrete the spermatophore casing—and hardens when exposed to the air. Prolonged matings assist the plug to set and also serves to hold the pair together during the sexual act. But there is sometimes a price to pay for imposing chastity. Besides blocking off the female butterly from further sexual engagements, the male's genitalia occasionally become glued into the sphragis. When this happens he must leave most of his mating tools in the custody of his mate, and that puts an end to his sexual career. With luck they will have served their function.

Mere mechanical obstacles to mating are not foolproof. Males who can break the barriers built by previous lovers will have the advantage in the breeding business. Needless to say, vaginal plugs are not always wholly effective in preventing sperm displacement by second or third males chancing their luck. While females remain sexy, no male can bank on exclusive mating rights, no matter what bondage device he uses to block her rear approaches. That is why some male insects have exploited ways of leaving their mistresses chaste in mind as well as body once they have finished with them.

Aedes aegypti is one of the most notorious mosquitos in the world because it carries the virus of yellow fever throughout tropical Africa and America. The disease nearly brought the building of the Panama Canal to a halt, because of its debilitating influence on the work force. The malignant virus was spread by millions of pregnant mosquitoes rising from swamps and thirsting for blood to nourish their eggs. In tapping the veins of their human hosts like hungry vampires, they gave their blood donors deadly shots of yellow fever. The female *Aedes* are totally single-minded in their quest because once they have been impregnated their thirst for sex vanishes. The males see to that by slipping them a sexual sedative in their semen. The active ingredient appears to be a hormone that is rapidly absorbed through the vaginal walls, then infiltrates the female's nervous circuitry, and there switches off her urge for mating. As a bromide, the hormone is exceptionally potent; an extract from one male is sufficient to make no fewer than sixty-four females completely frigid. The nerves controlling the vaginal lips may be the target for the male's anti-sex substance, because after her first sexual fling the female keeps her rear entrance firmly shut against all comers.

Sophisticated hormone treatment does not exhaust the male insect's ingenuity in deterring promiscuity. Monogamy in Heliconid butterflies is also a matter of chemistry. These eye-catching beauties, their velvet-black wings gorgeously decorated with splashes of red, yellow, and orange, live in the American tropics. They flaunt themselves brazenly in forest glades because their juicy bodies are protected by poison—a fact they cannot afford to keep secret. Birds ignore the warning coloration at their peril, because the butterflies have a nauseous taste and, if tampered with, emit a filthy stench. During the act of love, the male douses the female's erotic perfume by smothering her with an offensive-smelling scent so strong that even humans can detect the repulsive body-odor of the mated females. On other male Heliconids its effect is very specific. The scent contains an airborne hormone that acts as an antiaphrodisiac, so that when the couple part the stinking female is given a wide berth by other males. Nevertheless there is a puzzle to be solved, because the females themselves connive with their lovers, having special "glands" to take on the ill-smelling fluid. The females also possess a pair of "stink clubs," abdominal structures which fit neatly into a pair of glandular pouches on the male during copulation. So, although the male's technique looks like something out of a dirty-tricks campaign, being made to lose her sex appeal along with her virginity must somehow be in the female's interest too; otherwise she would not have developed reciprocal structures to aid the scent transfer.

Mating monopoly is so important for males that many insect lovers pay the supreme price as they attempt to buy exclusive reproduction rights with their mistresses. Take drone honeybees for instance. Although sharing a hive with millions of females, drones must lead a frustrated life, because their feminine companions are utterly sterile and are programmed only to toil. Even the queen, all passion spent, has no more need of sex. The best the drones can hope for is the emergence of a new fertile queen who will briefly need their services in the sky, which is where bees have it off. When the long-backed virgin wings away from the hive on her honeymoon, she leaves a whiff of aphrodisiac behind her which drives the drones wild with desire. The competition among them is intense, and they pursue her like hounds following a fox's scent. There the similarity to hunting ends. In the nuptial flight of bees, only those who successfully intercept the quarry and take part in the royal gang-bang are in danger of losing their lives. For drones, copulation is nothing short of catastrophic, at least in purely personal terms. In order to lock into the royal rump, the male has to evert his complicated genital equipment (including his "penis") and this alone seems to cause paralysis, and within a short time death. His first act of love is inevitably his last. Not that a drone is much use afterward anyway, because his penis doubles up as an explosive bolt which serves to eject him after he has ejaculated. The separation is usually so forceful that the tip of the "penis" is torn off and remains behind in the queen's sexual passage.

Yet the drone's violent departure is not simply a macabre act of self-mutilation. Opportunities for sex are few for male bees, and so when the chance does present itself they must stop at nothing to grab it. Drones that leave their "penises" to the queens as mating mementos have an advantage, because the detached tips seal in their sperms, protecting them from being displaced by subsequent copulations. In the life game the fact that the drones lose their phalluses and die matters little; in dying they ensure that their genes are passed into the next generation.

Lethal sex is not uncommon. It is found in a familiar family of flies called the ceratopogonids, the notorious biting midges. Clouds of these can turn romantic walks by willow-fringed rivers into sheer misery during balmy summer evenings, when the females sally forth from the vegetation to suck blood. Females of *Johannseniella nitida* are Machiavellian, their desire for food continuing undiminished right through their act of lovemaking. Each is equipped to kill with a pair of jaws like scissor-blades: these they use to stab their victims, and unfortunately for the males they too fall into that category. After the male has made genital contact, the female turns on him like a heroine in a melodrama defending her honor and stabs him to death. Her preoccupation is of course food, not honor, and she sets about tucking into her lover's twitching body. However, his genital apparatus remains attached to her rear, acting as a very effective mating plug. Through self-sacrifice the male ensures the future chastity of his hungry heartless wife, and sees to it that he fathers her children.

We have all symphathized at some time or other with the appalling dilemma of the male praying mantis, who is driven by instinct into the arms of his femme fatale. Mantises are wonderfully skilled hunters designed for snatching and snaring insects in an instant with a flick of their viciously spiked forelimbs. When a female finds a hunk of man-mantis on her back, well within arm's reach, the temptation to collect an easy meal is too much. More often than not she flings a murderous arm around his neck and chews his head off as an appetizer. Losing his head in love may be part of the male's sexual strategy, for it isn't required to mastermind the act of sexual union. That is controlled from a nervous center way back toward the tail. While the female nibbles away at her lover, his rear portion continues the intimacy, oblivious of the catastrophe up front. For the mantis, self-sacrifice has been the best way of breeding at the expense of rival males. From the female's viewpoint, sexual cannibalism is not ghoulish, just practical sense. Once the male has linked up with her genitalia and commenced inseminating her, he has fulfilled his purpose and becomes disposable. By eating him, she uses the goodness of his body to nourish their joint brood and so help the survival of their genes. The females of some spiders engage in "manslaughter" for similar reasons.

Such bizarre sexual strategies suggest that for some species males are only useful for mating. Once they have delivered their goods they are useless. It's not difficult to see why. The future of a species lies with the fertilized females. Whatever food is around should be invested for their nourishment, not wasted on their now-superfluous lovers. Since the next generation will inevitably contain new males, why expensively maintain this year's model? Many species do not and have developed disposable males who self-destruct after sex.

If sex be sinful, then the males of many beasts receive their wages in full even without the help of femmes fatales. Sometimes death is caused indirectly, as with droop-snouted Saiga antelope from the Russian steppes. The stags are so rump-struck during the rutting season that they have no time for food; after their orgy in the autumn they are lean and exhausted, and most die when the bad weather sets in. In contrast the hinds keep their heads down low where the grass is, and are fat and healthy for the winter. Many fish die soon after spawning. Occasionally female salmon live to breed again, but their lovers invariably expire after spawning. Sex is usually lethal in spawning squid and octopuses.

We can be thankful that the concept of the throwaway male is rare in mammals. Nevertheless one exponent is known, from the Antipodes—where all sorts of interesting things happen in nature. Male marsupial mice *Antechinus stuarti* suffer dearly for being unique; they experience the ultimate anticlimax. If these marsupial mice could read their future in the stars they would live in dread of the southern spring, because beyond then they have no prospects of survival. Their frenetic mating jamboree is held about that time for three or four days, and after they have done their duty they die—every one of them. Postmortems have revealed that the males are wrecked after their affair, with infections, failed livers, hemorrhages, and ulcers. Precisely what triggers the widespread damage was an enigma until recently, when some biologists working on the problem at Monash University, Melbourne, elucidated part of the answer. They found that the life expectancy of male mice could be greatly extended by enforced celibacy. So it was concluded that the sex act itself somehow killed them. Copulation triggers a fatal surge of corticosteroids; a similar event precedes death in animals exposed to severe stress, such as overcrowding. All the males are abruptly removed from circulation, making it easier for the females and their litters to survive. The puzzle is that so few mammals use the same technique. Luckily for humans, our ancestors found that males have other uses as well and can pay their way in biological terms. Nevertheless, the fate of *Antechinus* should be a warning to male egotists everywhere: in the life game, oddities have a habit of becoming fashionable.

Even so, sex has its dangers for humans. Although admittedly the odds are low, we all run the risk of death during or immediately after intercourse, particularly when indulging in "illicit" sex. Passion, especially when spiced with a touch of guilt, drives up the pulse rate to nearly 120 beats a minute and raises the blood pressure to such an extend that even perfectly fit lovers can suffer headaches afterward. Less healthy people may become stricken with chest pains—or angina—or worse. According to a Japanese survey of the causes of 5500 sudden deaths, six women and twenty-eight men died from heart attacks after making love, one unfortunately on the first night of his honeymoon! Of the men, no fewer than twenty-one had just had intercourse with someone other than their wives. One needs to be fit to fling oneself into an affair of the heart!

The dwindling male is another solution to sexual economics. Dwarfs demand fewer resources because they eat less; they may even prefer a diet different from that of their larger females, and so not compete with them. Bondage between these odd couples is often thrown in for good measure, especially when the opportunities for meeting are few, and so ensures that affairs last a lifetime. This happens with at least four kinds of angler fish, which inhabit the vast black void of the deep, where life is sparsely scattered. The relationship between the sexes is a very close one, because the ogrous meter-long females take possession of their thimble-sized husbands, and the two become as one flesh. The young bachelor fish swim freely around, but if one is lucky enough to come face to face with a female angler of the right kind, he anchors himself by means of a ravenous lovebite, sinking his needle-sharp teeth in her body. Then an extraordinary process takes place. Once the dwarf lover has made himself fast, he slowly loses his individuality, as his flesh slowly merges with hers, until he even comes to share her blood supply. It is almost the ultimate extreme of female liberation because the male is finally reduced to a degenerate serf bonded for life to his mistress, obediently shedding sperms when she feels like spawning.

The details of the deep-sea angler's sex life long remained a mystery; it was widely held that they had none, because all the individuals trawled up from the abyss were females. The amazing truth was only discovered when someone took a careful look at the small fleshy "growths" on the females' bodies and found that they were parasitic males—each female carrying around up to half a dozen of them. The female has dispensed with the bother of finding independent-minded husbands at spawning time and having to compete with them for food, and accordingly has become what amounts to a self-fertilizing her-maphrodite.

The ultimate economy is to do away with males altogether, for females to lead celibate lives without the complication of sex. Several quite advanced animals have dispensed with the sexual connection.

Virgin birth, or reproduction via unfertilized eggs, is a common strategy among insects such as termites, bees, ants, stick insects, and aphids. For them it has an enormous advantage, because an all-female species can reproduce twice as fast as a population of similar size in

which half the individuals are males. During periods of expanding
food supplies it makes economic sense to forget carnal pleasures (if
these insects can have them) and reproduce asexually. Aphids carry
on—and on—like this during spring and summer, as gardeners know
only too well. As the sap rises and the plants grow fast, the greenfly
goes celibate. Each female becomes an assembly line. The pestiferous
black bean aphid gives birth each day to twenty-five daughters who
will keep their virginity but within a day or so will themselves each
give birth to more females. The potential for population increase is
enormous. So is the price, because virgin birth is achieved at the cost
of genetic variability. Being genetically similar, mothers, daughters,
and granddaughters are as alike as peas in a pod; they are literally
chips off the original old block. Where individuals differ among themselves the species has an insurance against future changes in the
environment. That is why aphids and stick insects revert to sex every
twenty generations or so—to put the much-needed variety back into
life.

No such reversion has been recorded for vertebrates which indulge
in virgin birth. The first authentic case of virgin birth was recorded
in 1932 when Texas mollies—the fish *Poeciliops formosa*—were found
breeding without the aid of males. In 1935 an eminent British her-
petologist, Dr. Malcolm Smith, noted a curious thing—that the Indian
gecko *Hemidactylus garnoti* was only known from female specimens.
Twenty years later a Soviet zoologist, J. Darevsky, carrying out
fieldwork in the Caucasus, collected more than 5000 specimens of the
lizard *Lacerta saxicola* but failed to discover any males. He solved
the riddle by carrying out a detailed research program and showed
that isolated females alone could lay eggs, from which mostly healthy
young females hatched. The occasional male was usually defective
and died. In 1958 it was noticed that whip-tailed lizards *Cnemido-
phorus tesselatus* from the Big Bend region of Texas were all female;
subsequent experiments confirmed that they also cope without copulating. A few males have apparently been discovered, but they are
so heavily outnumbered that virgin birth must be the general method
of reproduction. Since then many all-female societies of lizards and

snakes have been described, together with a handful of unisexual salamanders.

The frequency with which virgin birth turns up in animals as high on the evolutionary scale as reptiles sharpens the mind, and forces one to take it seriously. The lesson is that the male sex is not always necessary, even for quite complex animals. Sometimes at least, the future can be happily left to the females. As a species insurance policy it is superb for desert-island situations: no need for the lonely castaway to yearn for a mate, because soon she can start to populate the island all alone. In practice, whip-tails don't travel the high seas, but a female may chance across a vacant patch of countryside and fill it with her children without hanging around for a mate.

There are other approaches to self-sufficiency, nonvirginal ones involving both sets of sexual organs, but doing your own instead of someone else's thing. Bisexuality has been a subject of fascination from the time of the ancient Greeks, who appreciated bodily beauty as well as intellectual excellence. They viewed every person in a sense as double-sexed; this was expressed in their worship of Hermaphroditus. This ambiguous god sported a beard and male genitals but dressed as a woman; he was sometimes given a pair of female breasts as a bonus. Despite their elevated status, these gods with mixed-up bodies were far from self-contained in their sex lives, because each was a hopeless muddle of male and female parts, half-man, half-woman. Sex is no good by halves. Human hermaphrodites— as the few people with ambiguous anatomy are called—are merely unfortunate victims of anomalous development, and can only be helped toward sexual happiness with the surgeon's knife.

Animal hermaphrodites are different, literally double-sexed by design and containing full complements of both male and female reproductive organs. Not that all are capable of mating with themselves. Most kinds of worms are bisexual, but their genital geography makes self-service impossible: every earthworm needs another to lie beside it on the lawn during the mating season, so that each can exchange both eggs and sperms. So do most hermaphroditic mollusks

and barnacles. After all, cross-fertilization reaps the benefits of sex, generating much-needed diversity in the offspring.

Nevertheless, some species can dispense with the genetic advantages of cross-copulation and service themselves. This happens with both free-living and parasitic flatworms. For a tapeworm, the survival value of being able to mate with itself, as it lives alone in its host's intestine, is obvious. The body is simply a ribbon of reproductive segments, continually budded off from behind the head. Each contains a full set of both male and female organs, with the "penis" and vagina opening alongside into a common genital pore. The arrangement seems convenient. But tapeworm sex is complicated by the fact that the male and female organs mature at different rates. The testes become operational and degenerate before the eggs ripen. This means that the young front sections are functionally male, whereas the older egg-bloated rear ones are female. Mating takes place by bringing the respective genital pores together when the ribbon becomes folded. For the broad fish tapeworm, which reaches a length of sixty feet and plays havoc with the digestion of people who live around the Baltic, autocopulation involves a mighty tangle.

Self-service sex is not always easy to prove, even when it is known that a creature is bisexual. For example, the flatworms that glide along the bottoms of ponds and streams like magic carpets practice cross-copulation. Each one has a protrudable penis that plugs into the vagina of its bisexual partner. An American species called *Curtisia foremanii* does however cope by itself. Proof was obtained in a laboratory by keeping them in lifelong solitary confinement. When mature, these loners produced fertile cocoons. These also were isolated and the worms that hatched out ultimately reproduced. Strict measures had to be taken to rule out clandestine matings, and the possibility of virgin births. After three generations of *Curtisia* had bred in utter isolation, the conclusion was drawn that these tiny living mats were doing their own thing. *How* they did it remained a mystery. Certain marine flatworms have been caught in the act of doing themselves, with their body neatly folded to bring the penis within plugging distance of the "vagina." Whatever method *Curtisia* uses, nobody has ever actually seen it being sexually self-indulgent.

A barnacle in the breeding mood is also a double personality. It can, as we have seen, act as both lover and mistress simultaneously. In fact it perfers to do so, by carrying on with one of its neighbors with the help of its pair of long-reaching penises. But there is a limit even to the barnacle's extension, and if potential partners are sadly stuck beyond the reach of each other's tools, unable to give mutual satisfaction, they occasionally resort to self-fertilization as a back-up breeding strategy. For common shore barnacles the world over, the critical mating distance appears to be approximately 5 centimeters, which may represent the maximum extension of the penis. That isolated barnacles often become gravid with developing broods shows that they can ejaculate internally and fertilize their own cargoes of eggs: an invaluable practice for those living greatly spaced out high on the shore or singly on the shells of mobile sea snails. The fertility rate is much lower than for those which cross-copulate, but then to produce just a few baby barnacles is better than to have none at all.

Some fish are self-fertilizing hermaphrodites. One of the strangest is a toothed carp called *Rivulus marmoratus* found in the brackish waters of south Florida, Cuba, and the Bahamas. Although the majority of toothed carps copulate, the males injecting sperms by means of a tubular anal fin equipped with grappling hooks, *Rivulus* has no need of company. Each fish is a self-contained production unit sporting a combined ovary and testis—an ovotestis. When the eggs are shed from the ovary, they have already been penetrated by sperms, their development guaranteed without the need for pairing. Pure males are occasionally captured, but they are rare although possibly useful in providing a little genetic variety now and again. But with so many self-sufficient hermaphrodites around, they can't have much fun.

Among the spawners, the sea bass include several bisexual species, such as the scribbled sea perch *Serranus scriba* from the Mediterranean. The most amazing example of dual sexuality, however, comes from the reefs of Florida and the Gulf of Mexico, where belted sandfish *Serranellus subligarius* become sexy in the late afternoon. Scuba divers interested in watching rather than spearing fish noticed something very odd about them, because the spawners had dual personalities and freely switched from one sex to another. One moment a fish appeared coyly effeminate, spawning in the company of males, the next she appeared to turn lesbian, changing her color and her sex act. On investigating, she turned out to be far from queer, because she eventually shed milt among the eggs of her female partners. As it happens, belted sandfish do not change sex. They don't have to. They simply play whichever role they feel like because each is truly ambisexual, with both male and female gonads—something that many of us would like to try out!

On the other hand, there are intriguing examples of species which go in for permanent sex reversal as part of their normal life-style, where it often appears to be a method of enhancing fecundity without incurring the genetic penalties of wholly dispensing with males. After all, it is the males that help to shuffle the genetic pack through sexual reproduction. In the case of the Red Sea fish *Anthias squamipinnis*, the vast majority are adolescents and spawning females. Mature males, holding territories along the tops of coral blocks, are few, but around in sufficient numbers to serve the female's sexual requirements. It has been found experimentally that "expensive" males are only "produced" if there is a need for them, that is if their density drops too much. Should this happen, a few females will change into males. Under this system, nearly every individual can produce fry by the thousands.

The slipper limpet *Crepidula fornicata* is one of the many mollusks that change sex. Those who have beachcombed around the flat muddy creeks of southeastern England or the northern coast of Holland and Germany will be familiar with the shells of slipper limpets. They have a peculiar habit of living in chains, formed by one animal settling on the back of another, and so on, until eight or nine cling together like a pile of inverted teacups. The chains themselves are a result of the limpets' unusual sexual needs. As the free-living young ones mature, each first develops into a male equipped with a large penis. When seized by the desire to put it to the test, the male is gripped by wanderlust and crawls until he makes contact with another slipper shell. If it is an older one, it is likely to be a hermaphrodite, sporting not only a penis but also a vagina. Extending his fleshy penis to the full, the settler wastes no time in feeling beneath the shell-shirt of his newfound mate for "her" agreeable sexual entrance. The best is yet to come, because the limpet has twice as much excitement in store. He gradually becomes refashioned as a female. As the transformation gets under way, his gonads start to make eggs as well as sperm, and a vaginal opening appears in his flank. At this halfway stage in the sexual refit, he/she will be mounted in turn by a younger male and feel an eager tumescent penis poking into his/her newly acquired female passage. For a time, the ambisexual slipper limpet delights in a double-decker relationship, being mistress to the male on top and lover to the one beneath. Double sex is disappointingly short-lived, and as the limpet grows on it becomes fully female. By the time she reaches the bottom of the stack—as those beneath her die—her penis has long since shriveled to almost nothing.

For the parasitic water louse *Lironeca convexis,* sex reversal is accompanied by a change of living quarters. Like slipper limpets, these small crustaceans start life as full-fledged males; they lodge in the gill chambers of certain kinds of mackerel. As the males grow, they suddenly move up front into the fish's mouth and become functional females in the process.

Hitchhikers and bothersome hangers-on like water lice are of special interest to the professional cleaner fish that advertise for infested clients around tropical shores. One of the most widespread is the black-and-blue-striped cleaner wrasse *Labroides dimidiatus,* for whom sex reversal is under social control. Anyone who has snorkeled around the edge of a coral reef will have noticed that cleaner wrasse are strictly territorial. Each lump of rock that emerges from out of the blue has its own bevy of laundrymen. Occasionally a scrap and chase disturb the serenity of the underwater scene as an intruder from a neighboring firm of cleaners is pursued through the tangle of stony sculptures.

Aggression plays a key role in the wrasse's sex life. Each territory contains a tyrannical male who firmly dominates his harem of six or so wives. He has to, because only by continually demonstrating who's boss can he prevent one of them from changing sex and usurping his position of power. His females are not all that they seem; each is an undercover male! When approaching maturity these fish develop into hermaphrodites, but being young and inexperienced they join the harems at the bottom of the pecking order. Here they bear the brunt of everyone's aggression, which suppresses their masculine tendencies. Accordingly they become good wives. The chance to change sex and status comes with the death of the despot at the top. Within an hour or two of his disappearance, the most dominant female turns butch, becomes aggressive, and displays like her lost overlord. The switchover to male spawning takes a little longer, but within four days "she" will have completed the transformation to full male status, providing she is not taken over by a more dominant neighboring male during the transition period. If one of these turns up, he will soundly thrash her—fish style—and make her revert to being a submissive mistress.

The relationship between power and sexual status makes good sense. A female who asserts herself sufficiently to become the top-ranking member of the harem must be one of the most successful of her species. But as a female, her reproductive potential is limited. The only way she can increase her contribution to the next generation is to change sex, take over a harem, and fertilize eggs from several females. The logic of the cleaner wrasse's system is easy to understand; the mystery is, again, why more animals have not exploited the system.

Whichever way animals play the generation game, their techniques are nearly always related to the transcendent need to reproduce. Homosexual diversions are usually counterproductive, though not always. When females mimic males in sexual behavior they are sometimes simply gaining a reproductive advantage. Occasionally cow couples strike up what appear to be lesbian relationships in which one puts on a convincing lover-bull act. The cow mounts other females and imitates the action of a copulating bull right down to the pelvic thrusts. One of the twosome is usually in heat, which makes her behavior even more mysterious, since it is in her interest to attract a bull rather than play unproductive games. Possibly, however, sex acts between consenting females bring the bulls running. During the breeding season, cattle like many hoofed animals live in large female herds, usually with one overlord who will try and mate with each of them as they come into heat. But with such large harems, there may be a limit to the bull's awareness. If he is too busy to notice that a cow has suddenly slipped into estrus, he certainly won't fail to react to the sight of one of them being mounted. He may well mistake the butch cow for another steer threatening his dominance and investigate promptly. On closer inspection he will find out that it's only a couple of queer cows, but with luck one will be ready for his service. So, by playing at being a bull, a cow in heat may be able to rouse her lover more quickly than by simply playing coy.

Sodomy has been recorded from many kinds of animals. Male squid have been seen to engage each other in a sexual hug and successfully place sperm packets in each other's body cavities. Captive male lizards will also mate perfectly successfully with members of their own sex. Homosexuality is rife in wildfowl and fish, and sexual liaisons between male mammals are not unusual. Often these relationships can be explained because they occur in conditions of sexual deprivation, where female company is lacking. This happens in zoos, aquaria, and wildfowl collections, where all sorts of odd behavior patterns flourish. As males become more sex-starved, they start to accept substitutes. The nearest thing to a female may be a male of the species, especially a young male, probably more femalelike than a mature one. It is no accident that many men who cannot make it with women are drawn to boys, a situation that has a parallel in the animal kingdom, where bull bison, frustrated by waiting for the cows to consent, may ram the adolescent males. These do not sport the woolly

beards and capes that are the signs of bison manhood, and so resemble their mothers. In lizards, the sexes are outwardly very similar, both having that single rear entrance, so in the absence of choice a male may find another male a reasonable understudy for a lady lizard.

Very recently, naturally occurring lesbian relationships have been found in birds living off the coast of California. These unusual goings-on came to light when scientists surveyed 1200 nests of western gulls breeding on an isolated rock near Santa Barbara, just forty miles north of Los Angeles. They found that quite a lot of nests contained about double the normal number of eggs. On closer investigation, it turned out that the nests with abnormal clutches were occupied by all-female "pairs," and to their astonishment accounted for 10 per cent of the gull population at this particular colony. The birders concluded that this state of affairs was caused by a shortage of cocks, so it paid the hens to go lesbian for the season, relying upon roving adulterous males to inseminate them and teaming up with another hen in a similar predicament with which to share nest duties. In this way, at least they would stand a chance of rearing a chick or two rather than remain barren for the summer.

Sex between consenting male mammals is technically more difficult. The only way open is anal intercourse. Even in heterosexual situations, male lovers occasionally hit an erroneous zone: tomcats may wind up pussy-whipped by thrusting away into their females' rears, and bull Indian elephants have been witnessed making rectal contact and ejaculating into their cows' back entrances.

In the complete absence of suitable sexual partners, or in the case of badly socialized individuals, masturbation may take over as the only alternative. Surprisingly, going solo is not such a rare phenomenon in our subhuman cousins. Some accounts have already been given. Furthermore, both sexes practice it. Female mammals in peak heat may resort to rubbing their sensitive genitalia rhythmically on the ground or on sharp projections, thus creating the stimulus of a penis jerking in and out. Female cats regularly resort to this kind of simulated intercourse. In the farmyard, boars massage their penises against the floor, stacks of straw, or other objects.

Some "fetishes" are easy to understand, because the objects have something in common with a real mate or companion. A bottle-nosed dolphin frequented the southwest coast of England and delighted holidaymakers with his friendly frolics. Boats held a special fascination for him, particularly rubber dinghies, which he tended to nuzzle and rub against. If only the tourists knew what was really happening down below! Those who looked carefully at his behavior saw that the dolphin was not merely scratching his back against the hull but was sexually aroused. When making contact with the boat, his massive pink penis was usually unsheathed and he then masturbated against the hull. Dolphins are normally sociable, but this one was for some reason an outcast, craving for company. Since no other dolphins were around, perhaps rubber dinghies with their gray dolphinlike skin were his next best form of comfort.

Bulls commonly practice autoeroticism by arching their backs and thrusting their fibroelastic tools in and out of their sheaths. This generates sufficient stimulation to cause a release of semen. Most primates are ideally built for self-sex, with their loose swinging arms and nimble fingers. Male monkeys and apes regularly masturbate, even when attractive and sexually active females are available to them. They use a variety of methods to achieve satisfaction, such as making pelvic thrusts into the ground. Some may even be able to perform the incredible contortion of self-fellatio, mouthing their own penises. Male monkeys were also the first exponents of the "five-knuckle-shuffle," in which the erect penis is loosely clasped by the hand doubling as a substitute vagina. Females are no less dextrous than their mates, and masturbate when they feel like it by tweaking their clitoris. Little female talapoin monkeys from the mangrove swamps of equatorial Africa may even finger themselves through their back legs while holding their normal sexual-presentation posture. As they become more excited, they make the same cries and grimaces as they would during a real copulation with a male.

Since we belong to the most sexually active species in the world, it should come as no surprise that men and women are the most accomplished practitioners of autostimulation. Masturbation is a form of experimentation for both adolescent boys and girls. It can even take the form of sexual contests. For example, it has been reported that gangs of Amerindian Crow youths engage in finger-frigging parties to measure their erect penises and to bet on each other's ejaculation distances. Such games are not unknown in the dormitories of boys' schools. From the surveys so far conducted, and there have been many, it can be safely assumed that by the age of twenty-five, more than 90 per cent of all men have regularly masturbated, and 70 per cent of women have frequently brought themselves to sexual climaxes. Apart from massaging their private parts with their fingers, women through the ages have used all manner of objects as stand-ins for the real thing.

Despite its prevalence and the fact that it appears as a reasonably normal form of sexual outlet in advanced animals, masturbation has been bedeviled by more humbug in Western civilizations than any other form of sexual activity. This stems from the ancient fear that the human race could become extinct if lovers refrained from pro-creating. Religious teachers accordingly sought refuge in the Bible, and roundly condemned sperm wastage as the sin of Onan (thus *onanism*)—he, it will be recalled, refused to have children by his brother's widow and at the crucial moment spilled his seed onto the ground. Since then, there has been confusion in the minds of God-fearing men between the equally harmless practices of masturbation and coitus interruptus. The story is still put around that boys who resort to self-consolation risk blindness, insanity, instant loss of memory, or life-sapping diseases.

Although repugnant to most people, human intercourse with animals is perhaps more widespread than one might think. Fishermen off the African coast near Mombasa make it with mermaids. They are not to be envied this form of bestiality, because the mermaids are far from the bewitching beauties who—according to legend—gave seamen the eye and lured them over the gunwales to their doom. These mermaids are sea cows or dugongs. Admittedly, the females proffer a little bit of appeal, having shapely breasts similar to those of women, but otherwise they are ugly when judged by our standards of sexual attractiveness, with faces fit to sink a thousand ships—or to shrink the most determined erection. The Kenyan fishermen, undeterred, catch them, haul them aboard their boats, and commit sodomy on the dead or dying sea cows. Live beasts make better stand-ins as sexual partners. All over the world, men have independently found that a mare is a passable substitute for a woman. Accordingly those, like the Masai, who feel that practice makes perfect in lovemaking regularly chance being kicked where it hurts and go to work on donkeys. But in Europe and North America, bestiality is greatly frowned upon today. The odd farmhand occasionally achieves notoriety in his local court, accused of being caught in a compromising situation with a cow. Such goings-on must have been commoner in Merrie England, because Henry VIII saw fit to find time between sorting out his own marital difficulties to pass a bill proclaiming bestiality a felony. Not that women are blameless. Horse-riding is not always simply a country pursuit. Intercourse on horseback is attributed to equestrian peoples like the Tartars and gauchos, where the man controls the animal and the girl sits astride but facing him. Taking horses and asses as lovers goes back to the ancient Greeks and Romans, who were fascinated by couplings between humans and animals. Even today, curiosity in zoophilia is by no means dead; bestiality magazines flourish.

Dogs are different. If brought up from puppyhood in the company of people, they come to reject their own kind in favor of their masters and mistresses for all things. We have all experienced the attentions of a persistently frustrated hound greeting everyone with an ever-ready erection. With a little help, sexy humanized dogs can be made to mount their mistresses. They can also be used as lap dogs. In theory, there is no limit to zoophilia. After all, we mate far more for pleasure than for procreation, and so men can find satisfaction in the mouth of a skate and women with the tail of a snake if they are that way inclined. A South African gentleman is even on record as leaving his wife for a crocodile!

Otherwise, however, it is difficult to find meaningful examples of coupling between different kinds of animals. Where they do occur, they are usually between closely related species. Horses may strike up sexual relationships with donkeys, lions with tigers, and so on. In the life game they are not encouraged, because such liaisons result in infertile and maladaptive offspring. The bitterling's sex life is as bizarre as any interspecific relationship. The bitterling, a European freshwater fish, needs the service of a swan mussel in order to breed. Bitterlings are basically spawners, yet both sexes go through the motions of mating with mussels. When ready to couple, the male

bitterling courts his fat-bellied bride and leads her to the gaping valves of a freshwater mussel. She trails from her vent a long egg tube, and when she is ready to spawn thrusts the tube, up to the hilt, into the mussel's fleshy slit. The idea is to make use of the mussel's gill cavity as a brood chamber. In a second she withdraws, and this is the signal for the male to follow in her wake. He has no penis, merely a pimple, so he darts in behind her, settles his rump into the gap of the shellfish, gives a rapid wriggle or two and injects some semen.

It is in the bitterlings' reproductive interest to make love to mussels; this cannot be said for bees and flies, which visit prostitutes. In the animal kingdom, males rarely have to give bribes or offer favors in order to copulate, so cases of prostitution are hard to find. Very occasionally female monkeys turn into whores, peddling their sexual wares in return for the only currency that matters to them—food. But nature's best red-light districts include meadows and pastures, because that is where a few remarkable kinds of orchids are on the game.

The exotic flowers of orchids have always had sex appeal, some more than others. In 1745 the Swedish botanish Carl von Linné recorded that the flowers of *Ophrys insectifera* so closely resembled flies that a casual observer might actually believe one was squatting on the stem. The flower of the fly orchid—as it is called—is not alone in mimicking an insect. Several are beautifully designed like resting bees and wasps. They are so convincing as dummies that there just had to be an explanation. After two centuries of fruitless theorizing, botanists finally came round to watching what happens in the field, and they made an astonishing series of discoveries. Insects usually visit flowers to collect nectar and, in return, cross-pollinate them. However, these orchids have no nectar to offer. Far from being a refreshment bar, each orchid bloom is like a brothel, soliciting business from certain kinds of male bees and wasps. Each kind of orchid attracts its own clientele. The chief sex-seeking visitors are male mining bees, horned bees, digger wasps, and dagger wasps. One Australian orchid, *Cryptostylis*, caters for ichneumon flies. The males mate, and in return perform a service to the orchid by bringing pollen

sacs from another flower. In color, conformation, and size, the brazen blooms are excellent surrogates for sex. Indeed, in some ways they are better mistresses for the pollinating species than the real females. Some *Ophrys* flowers even produce a scented aphrodisiac which brings in the males more effectively than a real female's sexual odors.

Erotic perfumes are enormously important in sex appeal—even in ourselves, if we care to admit it. "I don't know what she sees in him," we say. The truth is she probably doesn't, but is infatuated by his body-odor. It happens even in the most refined circles. The fragrance of oranges played no part in attracting Charles II to Nell Gwyn; he dearly loved her for her smell of stale sweat. Josephine's brand of odor was much to Napoleon's liking; when planning an assignation, he would forewarn her not to wash for a day or two beforehand. Whether we like it or not, we naturally smell, and furthermore we probably all smell different. Our special scent-producing areas are situated beneath our armpits and around our genitals, and since these places are equipped with hairy tufts from which secretions can be evaporated and so spread around, our bouquet must be meant for our close companions. The effect can be devastating. Many women claim to be turned on by men's musky body-odors. Indeed, there is evidence that women have a nose for musk and that their sensitivity varies during the course of their menstrual cycle.

This variation certainly occurs from a substance called exaltolide, chemically related to the aphrodisiac made by boars to excite their sows. Men, young boys, and girls are completely insensitive to the stuff, but sexually mature women have no trouble detecting it, especially around the time they are fertile—which is to be expected if the airborne spices produced by men have any meaning. Men occasionally seek help from African and Indian civet cats, which produce musk in a pair of pods just beneath their tails. Of honeylike consistency, it can be spooned out of the pods, and at full strength creates an unpleasant stench. But the perfume industry has always had a high regard for "civet" and animals have been kept for scent collection, particularly in Ethiopia: when carefully blended, the musk has an agreeable scent of considerable sex appeal to humans—if King Solomon is anyone to go by. He was a great admirer of Ethiopian perfumes, and he did succeed in collecting 700 wives. In *Much Ado about Nothing*, Shakespeare makes Claudio remark that when a young man rubs himself with civet, he is in love. Although modern synthetic products have largely taken over from civet, it was long an important ingredient of perfumes for both men and women. So, in drenching their own musks, people were simply applying the diluted sexual scent of a super ferret!

The appreciation of sexual perfumes may be at the root of erotic games like genital kissing. Fellatio is not confined to human lovers. Female mammals occasionally investigate, and may even mouth and lick, the erect penises of their mates before or after copulating. Whether the males are directly aroused by the behavior is difficult to determine, because they are already committed to a course of intimacy. There is a worm that does the same thing.

Platynereis megalops is a bristleworm that forms spawning orgies in the plankton during its brief breeding season. When hosts of hot worms have assembled, the females develop a taste for males, and proceed to bite off their tails, which contain the sperms. Luckily, the lovers' front ends can swim away to regenerate, while the females tuck into their rears, sperms and all. Once the sperms have been swallowed and subjected to the stimulating action of the female's digestive juices, they burrow through the walls of her gut and make contact with her ripe eggs.

A form of fellatio is even practiced by some cichlid fish, such as *Haplochromis burtoni*. The females of *Haplochromis*, like those of several cichlids, have evolved a novel method of brooding their eggs—inside their mouths. They also need a novel means of fertilizing them. When the female cichlid spawns in company of a male, she spins around to take the eggs into her mouth, but she is often so quick off the mark in removing them that the male has no time to sprinkle his milt over them. Natural selection has provided him with an answer. He deceives his mate by means of "egg spots" on his anal fin. As she picks her eggs up, he flashes his anal fin in front of her nose and ejaculates. She grabs at the roundels as though they were real eggs, but all she gets is a mouthful of sperms. Fellatio is of course *not* oral fertilization, but the action is similar.

Comparisons between ourselves and animals are closer where cunnilingus is concerned. Females of all kinds of animals use erotic scents to lure lovers. Virgin moths are a case in point. Eighteenth-century naturalists noted with astonishment how male moths were apparently attracted from afar by newly emerged females of their species. Proof that a perfume was responsible came from France in 1879, when Jean Henri Fabre showed that a female moth under a glass hood was spurned by males that flew into his house, but that a piece of paper on which she had previously been sitting had magnetic appeal for them. The source of the scent is a pair of glands on the tip of the female's abdomen. Half a million female silk moths only contain 12 milligrams of scent, but the males are incredibly sensitive: half of the odor-receptors on the male's feathery antennae are tuned to receiving the single sex attractant made by the females of the species, and they respond virtually to lone molecules. When male silk moths detect the female's scent, bombykol, in the air, they become excited, flutter their wings, and fly off in search of the odoriferous virgin.

Unfortunately, this system lends itself to abuse, and the males of some moths find a female quite different from the one they were expecting. The magnificent spider of Australia has broken the chemical love code of the local female moths. She swings a sticky bolus for her supper. The globules on the end of her silken line smell just like virgin moths—a confidence trick that works, because the lovelorn moth males fly in and become tangled in the spider's whirling line. We too can use an insect's sex-attractant to lure it to its doom. Scientists have long planned to interfere with the sex lives of pests. The latest scheme on the domestic front is a come-hither perfume that may soon be the undoing of flies. It consists of poisoned granules that smell sweetly of muscamone, the come-on odor given off by ready and willing female flies. The males find the sexy scent irresistible, and buzz to their deaths.

Genital aroma is one of the major clues that help male mammals to assess whether a female is desirably ready to mate or not. These erotic scents spring from a number of places. The vagina is one of them, and males of many kinds use cunnilingus to "read" its message before attempting intimacy. Male rhesus monkeys can tell in an instant the sexual state of a female by simply nuzzling and licking her vagina.

Furthermore, if presented with a cold female, they can be cruelly deceived if she has had her rear smeared with the secretions of a female in heat. Although she reacts frigidly, her smell and taste say "come on," and smell alone is enough. Lone male monkeys step up their masturbation rate if they get a whiff of fertile females.

The vaginal perfume is both lure and aphrodisiac, and there is evidence that the attractiveness waxes and wanes with the sexual rhythm. After all, our private parts are more than simply aids to reproduction; the penis is both a sensual organ and a status symbol—which brings us to the socio-sexual connection.

8
The Social
Connection

If spotted hyenas had a sense of humor, the mere sight of each other would make for lingering chuckles. Of course jollity plays no part in hyena life. Their spine-tingling "laughter" has nothing to do with amusement; it is a sign of anger and often breaks out in the scavenging free-for-alls around the bloody carcasses of antelopes. Nevertheless, there is something funny—to us—about hyenas: it is nearly impossible to tell the difference between *his* and *hers!*

Although the males are fairly normal in their genital anatomy, the females are pure burlesque. Beneath the female's anus hangs a pouch filled with fibrous tissue, resembling her mate's scrotum. Her real surprise is her superelongated clitoris, which hangs from just below her vaginal slit. As if to emphasize its similarity to a true penis, she can extend and erect it at will. The riddle of the hyena's rump was an age-old puzzle—even the sage of ancient Athens scratched his head in bewilderment. Aristotle discussed the possibility that hyenas were hermaphrodites, and surprisingly this notion lingered on for centuries. It was not finally laid to rest until 1939, by the distinguished zoologist Leo Harrison Matthews, who later became scientific director of the Zoological Society of London. He took a close look at their hindquarters and demonstrated beyond doubt that spotted hyenas are just plain ordinary critters and come in two perfectly good sexes, but that the external genitals of the female mimic to an extraordinary degree the equipment of their mates. He remained perplexed as to why a female needs a pseudo-penis and a sham scrotum.

   That mystery was solved when naturalists went out into the East African savanna to see how they are used. One fact emerged straight away—the female's massive clitoris does not extend to the full when she makes love; in fact during intercourse she keeps it fully retracted. Whatever its function, they concluded it has nothing to do with courtship. Further sightings threw more light onto the problem. Full erections of both the male's penis and the female's pseudo-penis occurred in purely nonsexual situations—when hyenas encountered each other out on the plains. Genital erection was clearly part of a greeting ritual and took place irrespective of the sex of the individuals; even two females would exchange courtesies on meeting by lifting their legs and exposing their stiff clitorises to each other, their erections sometimes almost touching the ground.

   Ace hyena-watcher Hans Kruuk, who made a classic study of the spotted hyena clans living in the Ngorongoro Crater and the Serengeti, has attempted to interpret the significance of their genital display. Although most of us regard hyenas as rather scruffy refuse-disposal agents, they are also formidable predators. Like all killers in their class, they are equipped with massive jaw muscles and deadly slashing and bone-crushing teeth. These tools of their trade are lethal in more than one sense: while indispensable for slaughtering prey, they are antisocially murderous if unleashed in a fit of rage against a friend.

The control of weaponry has been a problem which all kinds of social predators have had to solve, from lesser black-backed gulls to lions. The hyena's solution is to display the genitals as a means of averting hostilities.

The technique works like this. Face-to-face confrontation is always likely to create trouble between edgy animals, if only because it brings opposing weaponry or teeth too close for comfort. But as they present their genitals for each other to sniff, their threatening heads are kept apart and facing in opposite directions until their mutual suspicions have evaporated. The females have fashioned a "phallic" display from their clitorises so as not to be at a disadvantage with males during tense encounters.

Originally the penis was used solely to pipe sperms into the female, and the clitoris was the female's prime erogenous zone. In hyenas they retain these functions but have also taken on another role, a nonsexual one, doubling as organs of social display. This kind of opportunism, which brings about a change of function, is very characteristic of evolution. Other examples come readily to mind.

The majority of mammals probably use urine for passing love messages. We have already seen how male porcupines spray their mates as a prelude to intimacy. When buck rabbits get excited in the presence of a passionate doe, they leap over her and direct a jet of toilet water at her. So do South American acouchis—but more precisely. Whereas the rabbit squirts backward and often misses, the acouchi stands up from behind and shoots forward through his erect penis onto the back of the female. Male guinea pigs and Patagonian hares—or maras—also perform the act of enurination.

Female mammals indicate their state of fertility by the levels of estrogen excreted in their urine. This is why males are often so keen on testing its bouquet, and may even nudge the rear of a potential mate to encourage her to urinate on their lips and nose. Male hoofed mammals adopt a special grimace—or flehmen face— while sampling the odoriferous cocktail, with their upper lips curled back exposing their gums and sensitive palate.

Sexual actions have been widely and extensively incorporated into the social language of animals. This social connection is no accident, because copulation itself has inherent qualities of command and submission. While mounted, a male has the female largely under his control—she may be partly trapped by his weight, held by his fore-limbs, and impaled on his penis. By contrast, when a female solicits sex and offers her hindquarters to a lover, she makes herself tem-porarily vulnerable to him. Since animal males are generally stronger and have higher social status than females, this is also an acknowl-edgment of dominance. These nonreproductive associations have gradually become major considerations in the social use of sex be-havior. So, when an animal wishes to submit and throw itself on the mercy of its superior, nothing could be more expressive than taking up a female sexual-invitation posture. A top-ranker can show off to others that he is boss by straddling his inferiors. The act of mounting and rump presentation are common social signals, expressing dom-inance on the one hand and appeasement on the other; and both sexes freely use the gestures in their everyday context.

Take rump presentation by mammals, for instance. Many mammals display flashy markings in their tail regions. They are most obvious in deer, antelope, and various kinds of wild sheep, on which areas of pale or white hair on the buttocks are occasionally framed to a greater or lesser extent by contrasting black stripes. Some kinds of antelope have erectile rump patches which are shown off by stotting—bounding stiff-legged with the haunches held high. Springboks spronk, dis-playing their specialized patch of long white hair by arching their backs and leaping into the air. The North American pronghorn has the most elaborate rump patch, with long pithy hairs all over its thighs and entire rear end. When displayed the hairs stand on end and resemble a pair of blooming white chrysanthemums—one on either side of the short black tail. They must be designed to draw the eye, but for what reason? It was always thought that they were follow-me signals, so that when the herd was in flight the laggers had the leaders' rear beacons to guide them, or the young could keep their parents in sight. The latest and most likely explanation is that the rump patches add visual impact to a calm-down or appeasement gesture based upon the female's soliciting stance. It works by offering a sexual target to an angry foe.

Making friends with and influencing high-ranking individuals is as important in other social animals as it is in ourselves. In practice, this means that a subordinate animal must be able to appease the temper of more powerful individuals. One of the best of the various ways of calming an uptight opponent is to divert his thoughts to sex. By presenting her colorful rump to a furious male, a lanky-limbed hind can take the wind out of his sails and remotivate his aggression into more friendly channels. What works for females can also apparently work for males. Over the course of evolution, they too came to fool their opponents by acting coy and adopting effeminate poses to signal defeat in the face of stronger animals. They accordingly evolved pretty "feminine" rump patterns, which once served solely to draw the male's attention to the female's vulva. If human males were to behave like subordinate bucks and stags, instead of showing a white flag of submission to a threatening superior, we would wave a pair of frilled panties in his face.

Having become part of the ritualized body language of many hoofed animals, in its social context the signal does not necessarily arouse sexual passions in the beholders. Their response is tempered by the situation. Monkeys and apes have exploited both their genitals and their mating actions for purely social purposes. Casual observers have always misinterpreted the high level of so-called sexiness in baboons and monkey societies. Naïve naturalists of earlier days thought that our cousins were lascivious degenerates, devoted to sexual depravity. Yet much of what so offended them was sham sex, concerned with maintaining the social order within the troops.

Those who regularly visit zoos will know that many female primates have extravagantly colored vaginal lips and buttocks which swell amazingly in rhythm with their sexual cycles. Deprived captive specimens often develop supernormal swellings in midcycle, often to the discomfort of the female and occasionally to the embarrassment of visitors. At the end of the last century, a forlorn Formosan rock macaque kept in the London Zoo became so inflated in the height of her heat that she was regularly removed from the public gaze for decency's sake. But of course the tumescent expanses of naked red or pink flesh are not meant for human eyes. The female's bulbous bottom is an erotic display, which she uses to attract her lovers. The males find her sexually most desirable when fully inflated, which is during the period when she is ovulating and therefore most likely to become pregnant.

Even when flat, the glaringly obvious come-on displays are used like handshakes, as appeasement gestures to high-ranking companions regardless of their sex. When a monkey swings its bottom at you, it is simply saying "I'm friendly and mean no harm." Charles Darwin, who pioneered work on the facial expressions of animals, knew that primates use their buttocks as social signaling devices. But females not only present to dominant males, in order to keep on neighborly terms with them, but also flash their pink genitals to more dominant females as well. For example, if an "aunt" baboon wishes to inspect a mother's tiny infant, she can do so only by observing the correct primate etiquette, signaling her friendly intentions with her blushing rump. In this way the mother's tendency to be overpossessive and hostile may be suppressed. Males also display the same good monkey manners to each other, communicating their submission or readiness to be friendly by exposing their rears to their superiors. Among many kinds of monkeys and baboons the males possess buttock patterns that resemble the genital coloring of their females and so can be used as social gestures just as effectively.

"Sexual" mimicry of females by males takes an astonishing turn in gelada baboons, which live in herds in the high Simien mountains of Ethiopia. A male gelada is a distinguished-looking animal with an arrogant face, a tufted tail, and a great billowing mane of long brown and blond hair. His most unusual character is an hourglass-shaped patch of naked red skin in the middle of his chest, which accounts for his other name—the bleeding-heart baboon. The females wear the clues to the male's raw-looking chest, because they too have areas of bare skin in the same place. Those of the females are much more extensive, and are surrounded by a necklace of white blisters. Furthermore, the female's red pattern bears an uncanny resemblance to her sexual skin and blushes and swells synchronously with it. Even the central disposition of her pendulous nipples is a passable imitation of her vulva. But why should she possess a mock sexual skin on her chest? The habits of the species may provide the answer: geladas spend much time squatting. They even feed while sitting down, so concealing the usual important focus for sociosexual signaling. By self-mimicry, wearing a rump pattern on their fronts where it is easily displayed, the females have solved the problem. The males have followed suit and can make use of the female's rump pattern to signify friendship or appeasement by simply baring their chests.

Perhaps the most fascinating aspect of the social connection is what primates have achieved with the masculine side of sex. Mounting and mating are not only used in purely reproductive situations between monkey couples; they are frequently expressions of power and authority. Dominance mounting can be seen in all sorts of circumstances, sometimes in response to submissive rump presentations. For example, a female baboon may wish to grab a morsel of food very close to a top-ranking male. As she gingerly approaches him she meets his threatening stare by swinging her rump around and displaying her genitals. His irritation thwarted, he grips her back, straddles her pelvis, and hardly troubling to assume an erection makes a few thrusts before letting her go. Having "deceived" him with an offer of sex, she gets the food without violence. He in turn has his self-confidence reinforced in an enjoyable way without the risk of being damaged by a retaliatory attack. The motivations of the couple are mixed, as with a secretary who can gain favors by flirting with an amorous employer. Mounting even happens between male primates. After quarreling, victors often assert their rank by covering the hindquarters of their beaten rivals and performing a rage-induced copulation. Females do it in similar situations, the higher-status animals mounting their inferiors.

Sometimes dominance mounting is rather different in technique from a true sexual copulation. With Indian rhesus macaques, it is a matter of where the actor puts his feet! During proper sex, the male covers the female's vulva by climbing up her legs and gripping her ankles with his prehensile toes. By comparison, a dominance mating can be a lazy affair, the top-ranker simply standing behind his inferior and keeping his or her feet firmly on the ground.

Rape may be a form of dominance mounting, combining a fierce degree of aggression with sexual motivation. Criminal rape is nothing more than sexual assault, and not infrequently leads to the murder of the victim—the supreme act of oppression. Although taking a woman sexually by force has always been considered one of the ugliest offenses a man can commit, and therefore heavily punishable, rape has always been sanctioned during times of war. From time immemorial, soldiers have celebrated their victories on top of the wives and daughters of their defeated opponents. It is difficult to believe that sexual deprivation is always at the root of the rapings: more likely, sex is a means of humiliating the population, spreading a few of the victor's genes around into the bargain. Dominance mounting by men against men is rarer, although not unknown in human all-male groups—such as prisons and boys' schools. Among men, though, rituals like board-room meetings have largely taken over from sexually derived patterns of reinforcing hierarchies. (It is fair to observe that a male rhesus monkey would wonder why the company directors and vice presidents do not simply mount each other in rapid succession around the table! A person's rank would be far more quickly confirmed, simply according to who mounted him and whose back he in turn climbed upon.)

Erection is the very essence of male sexual dominance, and many a monkey demonstrates his authority simply by exhibiting a turgid penis. This can lead to misunderstandings if you are not on the same wavelength. When organ-grinders were a common sight on the city sidewalks, they were often accompanied by capuchin monkeys which greeted passers-by with the best erection they could muster. Although treated with disgust, their intentions were honorable; it was simply their way of saying hello to imposing-looking pedestrians. Phallic displays are especially characteristic of New World species like capuchins and squirrel monkeys. A common expression of dominance for a male squirrel monkey is to move up to a subordinate, cock a leg and thrust an erect penis into its face. The females also use the same gesture, and like female hyenas have paradoxical genitalia with a pseudo-scrotum and a superclitoris which is capable of enlargement. Howlers and spider monkeys, which swing around in the South American rain forests, may also use penile displays, because the sexes are difficult to tell apart by their genital anatomy, although the long pendulous clitoris of the females do not seem to be erectile.

Male marmosets use their big white scrotums. When threatening, a male turns around and, with his tail raised, presents his opponent with a good rear view of his black thighs, which serve to set off his ample white pouch as it moves backward between his legs. Some rodents use their testes for intimidation. The male guinea pig, for example, normally keeps his testes modestly tucked away inside his abdomen, but during courtship and while threatening they descend into the very conspicuous scrotum and are arrogantly exhibited to the opponent by performing a contortion act. In monkeys, the disappearance of the testes may also have a communication value. When an adult male rhesus macaque is frightened or overwhelmed by the too-close approach of a boss monkey, his testes may temporarily move upward into his abdominal cavity; his red scrotum then appears like a limp fold of skin. Very frightened men may even suffer the indignity of their testes shriveling to almost nothing—luckily this reverses when their confidence and composure return.

Male apes also get worked up when they greet each other. When two long-lost chimpanzee friends meet, one usually stands up while the other runs toward him. They fling their arms around each other in a humanlike display of emotion, but unlike two men in similar circumstances they have erect penises. Whether their pink erections have any value as man-to-man signals or are merely by-products of excitement is not clear. However there is no doubt that male chimpanzees do not mind their genitals being touched by friends. Indeed, it appears to be good manners in some situations. A subservient male can ingratiate himself with his superior by going up to him and, reaching beneath his torso, delicately fingering his scrotum. Perhaps he wishes to cash in on the dominant male's meal; by performing a gentle grope, he may be able to touch his superior for a fig or two.

There is no hint of homosexuality in this behavior. Indeed, the chimpanzee's scrotum-touching is strongly reminiscent of the "Sepik handshake." This ritual is enacted between men from the Sepik River area of Papua–New Guinea when they meet after a long period of separation. They express their mutual pleasure and general bonhomie by entwining their forearms while placing a hand on the other's nose and phallus. It is difficult to imagine a more touching act of reunion and fellowship. In a sense, it is a doubly meaningful gesture because these primitive people identify the nose with the penis—their vigorously designed carvings make this connection abundantly clear. A further ceremony involving touching the pubic region survives only etymologically, when we are asked to place our hand on the Bible and solemnly swear to give honest and truthful testimony. Once upon a time, a person was asked to take an oath in full public view on the testicles of the person to whom the pledge was being given. The Bible itself contains many accounts of swearing by the genitals, although in the translation from Hebrew euphemisms like "loins" have crept in to spare the blushes of priests and congregations alike. When Jacob asked Joseph to see to it that his body was interred along with his ancestors in the Holy Land—and not in Egyptian soil—Joseph was asked to seal his promise by putting his hand under the old man's "thigh." The idea of taking an oath in this quaint way was to uphold the implied threat that the unborn generations—those who arise from the genitals—would seek revenge if the person dishonored the pledge or bore false witness. The equivalent today would be to demand that our judges and heads of state should bare their thighs when they, respectively, hear evidence or receive testimonials from ambassadors.

As we have seen, the simple display of genitals by a top-ranking male may cause an underling to stand in awe of him. It is no accident that the males of many primates have prettily colored penises and scrotums. The African vervet monkey has a splendid scarlet tool beautifully set off by pastel-blue balls. Even when relaxed, the sacred baboon has a long limp penis of shocking pink. The male proboscis monkey which inhabits mangrove swamps in Indonesia has plenty to show off at both ends. His head sports a fleshy pendulous nose of magnificent proportions, and down below he has a vermilion penis, usually tightly distended. Bright structures are generally designed to be seen, and male monkeys and baboons seem to use their eye-catching phalluses as warning beacons, perhaps to tell members of alien troops to keep away. Every troop tends to have male lookouts or sentinels, who sit in conspicuous places with their thighs spread. Although the penis is usually retracted, too close an approach by an outsider immediately elicits a powerful and vivid erection. Such displays are a form of territorial marking and stem from the time when the ancestors of baboons and monkeys used scented urine trails to defend their freeholds.

Many primitive primates still do so today. The squirrel-like tree shrews, which represent the kinds of animals from which all primates are derived, dribble urine onto their hands, from which it gets transferred to branches wherever they walk. Nocturnal galagos and lorises also use the smear technique of leaving scent trails. The slow loris does not bother to palm its urine, but simply dribbles wherever it goes. As primates progressed, they increasingly switched from the night shift to being diurnal animals and gave up smell in favor of vision as a way of establishing land rights. Accordingly the penis changed from being a dull scent-dispenser into a vivid emblem flaunted to demoralize strangers and trespassers. The mandrill shows the most amazing development of this. He flaunts his penis colors on his face and has the distinction of being the most flamboyantly decorative of all mammals. The resemblance between his face and genitals is astonishing, although difficult to appreciate in practice, because the ferocious-looking overlords keep their private parts private. After all, why should they take the trouble of splaying the thighs when the show is mirrored on the massive muzzle? A mature male possesses a scarlet penis framed by a pinkish-blue scrotum and a tuft of orange pubic hairs. The pattern is repeated on the face, with the bright-red nose flanked by a couple of cobalt-blue swellings and a beard of orange-yellow fur. By this remarkable arrangement, the male mandrill automatically directs his intimidating warning wherever he gazes.

Human beings have come a long way from their monkey and apelike ancestors, and yet much of what we see in our primate relatives can be applied to ourselves. That itself is interesting. It has been suggested that the face of a mature man is an "echo" of his genitals, with the bulbous protruding nose mimicking the dangling penis. Of course, there are those who would say that this is merely a result of our especially fertile imagination seeking similarities where none really exist. Maybe so. But we have got a supernose and the symbolism between it and the penis has arisen independently and with great regularity in works of art in different parts of the world. Even the testicles are represented by the cleft chin, the flared nostrils or, in the Baga fertility masks from Africa, by the eyes. The similarity is made all the more striking by the wiry male beard, which resembles pubic hair in texture much more than the refined stuff that sprouts from the top of the head.

The reason for wearing genital echoes on the face is that men are still, like monkeys, using their penises—or penis substitutes—to symbolize their might, power, and status. The evidence is all around us.

Those who observe carefully will have noticed that, on the whole, men sit differently from women. Although women rest with their thighs tightly closed, men automatically lounge around like male vervet monkeys and baboons, with their legs apart. If they were as naked as nature intended, the posture would expose their crotch and genitals for all to see. It has nothing to do with courtship or impressing the fair sex, but is simply a form of body-bragging which comes naturally to the "cocksure" male and is part of a hefty legacy of behavior patterns we have dragged into the twentieth century from our wild past.

Thigh-splaying has been further developed in Tahiti in the interests of ceremonial—a fact that did not escape the notice of Captain James Cook when he brought the *Endeavour* into Matavai Bay in 1769. The lush islands, inhabited by 40,000 people as beautiful as their surroundings, seemed a Garden of Eden, but illusions that the smiling, friendly Polynesians were living in arcadian innocence quickly vanished. Sex was out in the open, much to the mariners' delight; uninhibited intercourse was entered into as easily as one would take a meal or drink. In the Tahitians' strictly feudal society, the most privileged sect, the Arioi or priesthood, which included both men and women, loved and conceived with gay abandon—and practiced birth control by strangling their newborn children. One of their favorite distractions was dancing of a particularly explicit kind, many of the routines being based upon hip-thrusting, and thus very reminiscent of intercourse. When performed by women, the sensual erotic dances brought sweat to the brows of Cook's sex-starved seadogs. But such disassociation of sexual thrusting from intercourse, and its incorporation into a partly social ritual, is something we are all familiar with, because modern dances are derived from copulatory actions. Some are more obvious than others. Depending upon the occasion, dancing partners can jig around apart—a kind of touch-me-not lovemaking— while at more intimate times the rituals become, as they say, "navel encounters without loss of semen." However, there is nothing in our dance-hall repertoires to compare with Tahitian all-male dances, in which the men line up and rhythmically flash their thighs by rapidly opening and closing them to a vigorous musical beat. Far from exciting and delighting the womenfolk with the prospect of making love beneath the frangipani blossoms, this is nothing short of a powerful display of masculine assertion, made all the more spectacular by its ceremonial form.

Though such rituals are not performed with erections, the image of a stiff upright phallus has long played a part in symbolizing male dominance in all kinds of cultures, and is used even today by men who live in the central Western Highlands of New Guinea. If the sight of an erect penis means anything, then an enlarged or superpenis will be that much more effective. The jungle men from Papua go around almost naked, but hide their penises in arm-length hollow bamboo stems called phallocrypts. These do not conceal their contents: quite the reverse. The phallocrypt is nothing short of a man's falsie, projecting from the genitals like an enormous erect penis. Some are so uncomfortably cumbersome that they have to be held up by a cord tied round the wearer's waist. Once a man has become mature and initiated, the wooden sheath is part of the everyday apparel; it nevertheless remains an object of considerable pride, often skillfully etched and cheerfully decorated with bright bird feathers. The men of Malekula in the New Hebrides also improve on their own penises by wrapping them in bandages, made from banana leaves, known as nambas—pidgin English for penis lovers—i.e., sheaths! Like the phallocrypts, the nambas give their owners the look of having a permanent erection of supernormal size.

Even European males took to wearing falsies during the Middle Ages; instead of discreetly concealing their genitals behind a "fly," penis and scrotum were enclosed in a codpiece, a sex purse or glove. It was far from utilitarian, and was ostentatiously shown as a sign of virility and one-upmanship. The sizes of codpieces swelled, and by the seventeenth century fashionable men were displaying embroidered and heavily padded sex pockets tailored as though to suggest a mighty erection lurking inside. But what for? Is penis erection, or at least symbolization of it, really an effective sign of dominance?

The notion may explain the magnificent pubic ironwork worn by knights. War has always been an occupation of kings and princes, and when properly dressed either for ceremonial jousting—itself a martial art—or for the "kill," their suits of armor were designed to make everyone stand in awe of them. When they donned armor even the most feeble-looking men were transformed into daunting opponents. All without exception exaggerated the size of the occupants, and the great plumed and visored helmets gave them merciless and scowling "faces." Some of these battle suits also incorporated armored codpieces of outstanding proportions covering the humble priveés of the owners. One on show in New York's splendid Metropolitan Museum was worn just over 400 years ago by a Bavarian duke, Albrecht V, and could if necessary accommodate a handsome hard-on inside his rampant codpiece. (Of course, an erection is useless when encased in steel!) However, as a demonstration of manly vigor it must have been an impressive sight as the good Duke swaggered around the parade ground. King Henry VIII's display of sexual weaponry was even better. One of his engraved codpieces was stout enough to do justice to his boast of being the finest warlord in Europe, and sowed the idea that he was very favorably endowed in that region of his anatomy. For several centuries the Tudor accouterments of war have been part of England's heritage and placed for safekeeping and public viewing alongside the Crown Jewels in the Tower of London. But such was the marvel of Henry's hefty codpiece that it was long considered one of the famous sights of the Tower, and during the eighteenth century was removed from the rest of the suit and exhibited in splendid isolation. At the time this caused considerable excitement, especially among the ladies of London, some of whom were so aroused by the spectacle of the royal wrought-iron erection that some were moved to break time-honored taboos of public decency and rub themselves against the chased tip. Others used the larger-than-life codpiece as a phallic totem. Women who were experiencing difficulties in becoming pregnant apparently came along and stuck pins into the inner silken lining in the hope that their actions would remedy their problem. When slung across the crotch of the Tudor king, the genital armor was probably meant more for the benefit of men than for women.

That men do feel they can threaten each other by hiding behind the image of a massive sky-pointing phallus is indicated by the Zuñi Indians of Mexico. When searching for clues as to how people interpret body signals, one trick is to look at the gods they worship. For example, a god of fertility is likely to encapsulate the very signs by which we recognize fertility: usually such deities are shown as heavily pregnant women, their breasts distended with milk. The Zuñi Indians are pugnacious warriors. They make their supplications to a suitably aggressive god, made in the image of a man itching to do battle, bristling with signals that they recognize as being fierce. Although sometimes the Zuñis' war god takes on a complex form, occasionally he is reduced to a simple pole from which sprouts a corkscrewlike structure representing an erect penis. There is nothing erotic about a war god, and these Mexican Indians regard an erect phallus as simply the very essence of a threat display, designed to terrify their rivals and put them to flight. This helps to explain the significance of a whole range of so-called erotic art from the past.

In the lovely rolling vales of southern Dorset in England is the shameless Giant of Cerne Abbas, an immense figure of a man hewn by the Romans out of the turf of a green hillside. His creators 2000 years ago gave him not only giant-sized genitals but, worse, an erect phallus. The more sensitive inhabitants of that part of Dorset continually complain about his blatant nudity, and would like to see his erection turfed in. Luckily, the giant's genitals are in the safe hands of the National Trust, and so they should be, because the Cerne Abbas giant is not the whimsical work of a pornographic landscape artist. More likely he is a monumental warning to encroaching neighbors: in addition to his sexual "weapon" he brandishes a club in menacing fashion. Today we misinterpret his message, because to us an erect penis is no longer awe-inspiring but is synonymous with sexual arousal. The well-traveled Roman legionaries who occupied the countryside when the giant was methodically cut out of England's green and pleasant land would have been in little doubt about the dual meaning of an erection. Their bawdy god Priapus, who symbolized fertility, always had a tight and mighty erection. Sometimes he was shown reduced merely to his genitals: these decorative appendages were mounted over doorways, like lucky charms, warding off evil spirits. In their purpose the erections of Priapus bore uncanny similarity to the ithyphallic herms of ancient Greece. Many of them were used as property markers. These herms, pillars of bronze or stone, were each surmounted by an aggressive-looking head and displayed a prominent set of male testicles and an erect penis on the front of the column. Although the genitalia on the sculptures are worthy of superstuds, in fact they are symbolic not of sex but of power, and were used as home guards and border stones. They were ancient no-trespassing signs, placed in situations similar to those of the sentinels of monkey troops.

Even today, a few people still have faith in the power of a phallus poised for action. In Bali, straw scarecrows with protruding penises guard the rice crops. Wooden erections from Nais warn away demons, and stone ones as tall as a man keep evil spirits at bay in Korea. For high-ranking men from southern Ethiopia, the smart thing to wear is a vertical penis on the forehead—a cocky status symbol.

Ithyphallic statues are one of a range of substitutes that we men have invented to take over from our hidden or inadequate phalluses. We have long since passed the stage of the vervet monkeys or sacred baboons, whose leaders can keep their manly self-confidence and cause the opposition to quake by exhibiting a good erection. But the top men, whether leaders of nations, religions, or armed forces, still need to keep discipline in the ranks, maintain authority, and hold respect. To that extent their problems are similar to those of a high-ranking male vervet monkey. The differences are due to scale, and it's not surprising that over the ages, such men as popes and presidents have sought a little help from phallic symbols of office to bolster their egos, impress the crowds, and bluff their rivals. Admittedly, the search for sexual symbolism is a facile exercise, fraught with pitfalls: substitute phalluses are everywhere if you choose to find them. A necktie can be seen to dangle as a sham penis; a sleek red sports car, a pop star's electric guitar, an M-15 rifle can all be symbols of male potency— or not. But it seems likely and only human for monarchs, prime ministers, and archbishops to wield maces and scepters, to wear phallic crowns and miters, and live and rule beneath magnificent domed roofs. Maybe these at least are direct derivatives of phallic threat.

We are indeed the ace exponents of social sex, and have largely divorced copulation from breeding. The Pill has seen to that! Figures alone speak for themselves. Over the course of her reproductive life a woman may have intercourse at least 3000 times, and yet if she lives in North America or the United Kingdom she will probably give birth to only two or three children, at most. Even if she had the maximum of around twenty, she would still probably mate several hundred times for each child born. We all know the reason: making love is fun. Compared with other animals, we lead hyperactive sex lives, because we as a species have exploited the sensuality of intercourse to strengthen the ties between particular lovers. The differences which distinguish our kind of intimacy from that of our primate cousins are largely connected with our way of personalizing sex. Most male mammals take a rear approach to mating, and since one rump looks much the same as another, they are not all that fussy about whom they copulate with. We are exceptional and mate face to face, and since faces are all different we come to associate intimacy with a particular special partner with whom we are "in love." Accordingly, our bodies are "designed" to make frontal lovemaking rather more satisfying than the old-fashioned rear-entry technique. After all, our sexual playthings—our erogenous zones—are worn on our fronts.

And there is a whole galaxy of them. There are voluptuous lips to kiss, earlobes to nibble, nipples to knead and suck, and down below a very forward-placed clitoris to manipulate and make contact with the man's mightily developed penis. Some of these are frequently artificially decorated to enhance their seductive qualities. If lips are labial mimics carried on the face, glossy red lipstick converts them into supermimics adding a hint of "genital" lubrication that comes with sexual arousal; the redness imitates the flush of blood, which comes with excitement. So does rouge on the cheeks. Personalized sex did create one problem, hiding from the man's view his mistress' erotic bottom, always a turn-on for male primates. However, with the limitless ingenuity of natural selection, it seems that women wear a passable imitation of their sexy buttocks where their lovers can keep an eye on them—on their chests, as an opulent pair of breasts, whose cleavage and firmness is often exaggerated with a little help from lingerie. Soft feminine knees and shoulders may also echo the mammary orbs. Mutual sexual satisfaction is also made all the more certain by extended periods of love play in which all kinds of body intimacies take place such as stroking, cuddling, fondling, and kissing. These we all once experienced when we were infants and the focus of our parents' lavish affections. Indeed, it seems that much of the love play which we think of as being exclusively sexual has been "borrowed" from our infancy. Human lovers also have more opportunity for sexual intimacy than any other animal by virtue of the fact that their sex drives are permanently in gear, more or less irrespective of the time of year, the state of the woman's sexual cycle, pregnancy, or even age. It is hardly affected by the fact that women are "castrated" during the menopause; this is probably a safety mechanism for ensuring that faulty forty- or fifty-year-old eggs are not fertilized, and hardly affects female interest in sex.

People retain their taste for mating by virtue of another human attribute, our ability to use our brain as our best erotic organ. By exercising it to the full, we can derive lifelong pleasure in exploring our potential in the mating game. Not that sex is always mindless in animals. In gorillas, for instance, it is not simply a matter of clockwork. Though males only show serious interest in copulating when the females are in estrus, the females do have their favorite lovers when circumstances allow and tend to be aroused more by some than by others. Furthermore, they vary their mating technique between front to back and front to front.

Humans are inherently extraordinarily sexy creatures, as we've seen. This is an evolutionary legacy which it seems pointless to deny or suppress. If you like, it is a solution to the problem of maintaining close relationships between couples for comparatively long periods while their children are growing up. Enjoying personalized sex is the sensual reward that keeps them hooked on each other. Moralists have repeatedly bewailed our high level of sexuality as decadent, and the debate over birth control is bedeviled by biological ignorance. It stems from the notion that sex is primarily for reproduction. We have continued the trend to social sex, so that intercourse is nowadays overwhelmingly about expressing deep affection for someone very special. And this may be the happiest product of evolution so far.

References

Alcock, J., Jones, C. E., and Stephen, L. "Location before emergence of the female bee, *Centris pallida*, by its male (*Hymenoptera: Anthophoridae*)," *J Zool* (2) 179 (1976), 189–200.

Aleksuik, M. "Manitoba's Fantastic Snake Pits," *National Geographic*, 148(5)(1975), 715–23.

Archer, M. "Some aspects of reproductive behavior and the male erectile organs of *Dasyurus geoffroii* and *D. hallucatus* (Dasyuridae and Marsupialia)," *Mem Qd Mus*, 17 (1) (1974), 63–67.

Asdell, S. A. *Patterns of Mammalian Reproduction* (Constable, 1965).

Avonson, L. R., and Cooper, M. L. "Penile spines of the domestic cat," *Anat Rec*, 157 (1967), 71–78.

Barlow, G. W. "Social Behavior of a South American Leaf Fish, *Polycentuus schomburgkii*, with an account of recurring Pseudofemale behavior," *The Amer Mid Naturalist*, 78 (1) (1967), 215–34.

Barnes, H., and Crisp, D. J. "Evidence of self-fertilization in certain species of barnacles," *J mar biol Ass UK*, 35 (1956), 631–39.

Beatty, R. A. "Parthenogenesis in Vertebrates in Fertilization," *Fertilization: Comparative Morphology, Biochemistry and Immunology*, ed. C. B. Metz and A. Monroy, Vol I (Academic Press, 1967).

Blom, E. "Male reproductive organs of farm animals," *Reproduction in Farm Animals*, ed. E. S. E. Hafez (Lea and Febiger, 1962).

Brawn, V. M. "Reproductive behaviour of the Cod (*Gadus callavias L.*)" *Behaviour*, 18 (1961), 180–97.

Burton, J. "Virgin birth in vertebrates," *New Scientist*, 334 (7 August 1973).

Cave, A. J. E. "The processus glandis in the Rhinocertodidae," *Proc Zool Soc London*, 143, 569–85.

Clark, E. "Functional Hermaphroditism and self-fertilization in a Serranid fish," *Science*, 129 (1958), 215–16.

Coe, M. "Observations on the ecology and breeding biology of the genus *Chiromantis* (Amphibia: Rhacophondae)," *J Zool*, 172 (1974), 13–34.

Dathe, H. "Vom Harnspritzen des Ursons (*Erethizon dorsatus*)," *Zeits für Sauget*, 28 (1963), 369–75.

Dixson, A. F., Scruton, D. M., and Herbert, J. "Behaviour of the Talapoin monkey

(*Miopithecus talapoin*) studied in groups in the laboratory," *J Zool*, 176 (1975), 177–210.

Drew, G. A. "Sexual activities of the squid *Loligo pealii*," *J of Morphology*, 22 (1911), 327–51.

Edwards, E. "Mating behaviour in the European Edible crab (*Cancer pagurus L.*)," *Crustaceana*, 10 (1966), 23–30.

Eisenberg, J. F., and Kleiman, D. "Olfactory communication in mammals," *Ann Rev of Ecol and Syst*, 3 (1972), 1–32.

——, McKay, G. M., and Jainudeen, M. R. "Reproductive behaviour of the Asiatic elephant (*Elephas maximus maximus L.*)," *Behaviour*, 37 (1970), 193–225.

Fishelson, L. "Protogynous sex reversal in the fish, Anthias squamipinnis (Teleostei, Anthiidae) regulated by the Presence or Absence of a male Fish," *Nature*, 227 (14 July 1970).

Freedman, R. "Is sex necessary, or are we just stuck with it?," *New Scientist* (9 August 1973), 312.

Geddes, P., and Thomson, J. A. *The Evolution of Sex* (London, 1889).

Geist, V. "On the rutting behaviour of the mountain goat," *J Mamm* 45 (4) (1965), 551–68.

Ghiselin, M. T. "The Evolution of hermaphroditism among animals," *Quart Rev of Biol*, 44 (1969), 189–208.

Gip, B. *The passions and lechery of Catherine the Great* (Charles Skilton, 1971).

Guthrie, R. D. "A new theory of mammalian rump patch evolution," *Behaviour*, 37 (1970), 132–45.

Halliday, T. R. "On the biological significance of certain morphological characters in males of the Smooth newt *Triturus vulgaris* and of the Palmate newt *Triturus helveticus* (Urodela: Salamandridae)," *Zool J Linn Soc*, 56 (1975) 291–300.

——. "Sexual behaviour of the Smooth Newt, *Triturus vulgaris* (Urodela, Salamandridae)," *J Herpet*, 8 (4) (1974), 277–91.

Harrington, R. W. "Oviparous Hermaphrodite Fish with internal self-fertilization," *Science*, 134 (1961), 174–950.

Harrisson, T. *World Within: A Borneo story* (Cresset Press, 1959).

Hartnoll, R. G. "Mating in Brachyura," *Crustaceana*, 16 (1969), 161–81.

Herter, K. *Hedgehogs: A comprehensive Study* (Phoenix, 1965).

Hill, D. S. "Wasps and Figs," *New Scientist* (15 April 1971), 144–46.

Ingle, R. W., and Thomas W. "Mating and spawning of the crayfish *Austropotamobius pallipes* (Crustacea: Astacidae)," *J Zool*, 173 (4) (1964), 525–38.

Jackson, W. P. U., and Hoffenberg, R. "Sex reversal: Females with male nuclear sex," *Sex Differentiation and Development*, ed. C. R. Austin (Cambridge University Press, 1960).

Khalifa, A. "Sexual behaviour in *Gryllus domesticus L.*," *Behaviour*, 2 274.

Kleiman, D. "Scent marking in the Canidae," *Sympos Zool Soc Lond*, 18 (1966), 167–77.

Kruuk, H. *The Spotted Hyena* (University of Chicago Press, 1972).

Latta, J., Hopf, S., and Ploog, D. "Observations on mating behaviour and sexual play in the Squirrel Monkey (*Saimiri sciureus*)," *Primates*, 8 (1967), 229–46.

Lee, A. K., Bradley, A. J., and Braithwaite, R. W. "Corticosteroid Levels and male mortality in Antechinus stuartii," 209–20, *The Biology of Marsupials*, Stonehouse, B. and Gilmore D. (1976).

Locket, A. "A future for the Coelacanth?" *New Scientist* (1976), 456–58.

Lucie-Smith, E. *Eroticism in Western Art* (Thames and Hudson, 1972).

Maslin, P. "Parthenogenesis in Reptiles," *AM Zoologist*, 11 (1971), 361.

Maynard Smith, J. "What use is sex?" *J theor Biol*, 30 (1971), 319–35.

Michael, R. P. "Observations upon the sexual behaviour of the domestic cat (*Felis catus* L.) under laboratory conditions," *Behaviour*, 18 (1961), 1–24.

Michelmore, S. *Sex* (Pan, 1964).

Moorehead, A. "The Fatal Impact: An account of the Invasion of the South Pacific 1767–1840" (Hamish Hamilton, 1966).

Morris, D. "The behaviour of the green acouchi (*Myoprocta pratti*) with special reference to scatterhoarding," *Proc Zool Soc Lond*, 137 (4) (1962), 701–32.

Noble, G. K., and Bradley, H. T. "The mating behavior of lizards: its bearing on the theory of sexual selection," *Annals NY Acad Sc*, 35 (1933), 25–100.

Parker, G. A. "Sperm competition and its evolutionary consequences in the insects," *Biol Rev*, 45 (1970), 525–67.

Perry, J. S. "The reproduction of the African Elephant *Loxodonta africana*," *Phil Trans Royal Soc*, (B) 237 (1953), 94–147.

Rabb, G. B. "Evolutionary aspects of the reproductive behavior of frogs," *Evolutionary Biology of the Anurans*, ed. James L. Vial (University of Missouri Press, 1973).

Robertson, D. R. "Social control of sex reversal in a Coral Reef Fish," *Science*, 177 (1972), 1007–9.

Rosen, D. E., and Tucker, A. "Evolution of secondary sexual characters and sexual behaviour patterns in a family of viviparous fishes (*Cyprinodontiformes: Peocilidae*)," *Copeia* (2) (1961), 201–11.

Rothschild, M. "Fleas," *Scientific Amer*, 213 (6) (1965), 44.

Russel, W. M. S. "Experimental studies of the reproductive behaviour of *Xenopus laevis*," *Behaviour*, 7 (1954), 113–88.

Schaller, G. *The Serengeti Lion* (University of Chicago Press, 1972).

Schneider, D. "The sex-attractant receptor of moths," *Scientific American*, 28.

Shadle, A. R. "Copulation in the Porcupine," *Jour Wildlife Management*, 10 (2) (1946), 159–62.

———, Smelzer, M., and Metz, M. "The sex reactions of porcupines (*Erethizon d. dorsatum*) before and after copulation," *J Mammal*, 27 (2) (1946), 116–21.

Spieth, H. T. "Evolutionary Implications of Sexual Behaviour in *Drosophila*," *Evol Biol*, 157–93.

Wickler, W. *Mimicry in Plants and Animals* (Wiedenfeld and Nicolson, 1968).

———. "Socio-sexual signals and their intra-specific imitation among primates," 69–147, *Primate Ethology*, ed. D. Morris (Weidenfeld and Nicolson, 1967).

Wilson, E. O. *Sociobiology: The New Synthesis* (Harvard University Press, 1975).

Index